COMBAT KARATE

COMBAT
KARATE

JOSE M. FRAGUAS

DISCLAIMER

Please note that the author and publisher of this book are NOT RESPONSIBLE in any manner whatsoever for any injury that may result from practicing the techniques and/or following the instructions given within. Since the physical activities described herein may be too strenuous in nature for some readers to engage in safely, it is essential that a physician be consulted
prior to training.

First published in 2011 by Empire Books LLC.
Copyright (c) 2011 by Jose M. Fraguas.

Library of Congress Catalog Number:
ISBN-10: 1-933901-50-3
ISBN-13: 978-1-933901-50-3

Empire Books
P.O. Box 491788
Los Angeles, CA 90049
(818) 767-79 00

First edition
11 12 13 14 15 / 05 04 03 02 01

Printed in the United States of America.

Library of Congress Cataloging-in-Publication Data

Fraguas, Jose M.
   Combat karate / Jose M. Fraguas260
      p. cm.
   ISBN 978-1-933901-50-3 (pbk. : alk. paper)
   I. Title.
   GV1114.3.F714 2009
   796.815'3—dc22

2009023062

"One's blow always creates a kind of hollow. A blow is successful if, at the instant of impact, the opponent's body fits into that hollow space and assumes a form precisely identical with it."

— **Mishima Yukio**
Japanese writer

DEDICATION

I dedicate this book to the memory of Soke Mabuni Kenzo.

ACKNOWLEDGMENTS

Many people were responsible for making this book possible, some more directly than others. I want to extend my gratitude to all those whom so generously contributed their time and experience to the preparation of this work. A special thanks to designer Patrick Gross, whose flights of logic and guidance in the artwork of this book were always on the wings of excitement. To Patrick McCarthy and Avi Rokah for kindly allowing me to use their essays on kata and kumite as introductory chapters to this work. Your knowledge and expertise is greatly appreciated. I also want to thank France's Thierry Plee, long-time friend and president of Sedirep and Budo Editions; Mr. Schlatt, kind friend and founder of Schlatt-Books in Germany; Don Warrener, director of Rising Sun Productions; Harold E. Sharp, a true legend in the world of martial arts who kindly supplied great photos of his personal archives; and dear friend Isaac Florentine, film director and passionate karate-ka.

A word of appreciation is also due to my good friend Masahiro Ide, president of *JK Fan* and *Champ* videos, for his generosity and cooperation in this project; I also want to thank the publishers of *Gekkan Karate-do* magazine (Fukushodo, Ltd., Japan), for their assistance, kindness and supply of great photographic material for some of the chapters. Without their support, kindness and commitment to preserve the art of karate-do, this book would not exist.

And last but not least, to all my instructors, past and present, for giving me the understanding and knowledge to undertake all the martial arts projects I've done during my life. My understanding of the art has grown over the years, thanks, in great part, to the questions they made me ask myself. These questions—both perceptive and practical—have sent me further and deeper in search for answers. This book would not exist without you.

You all have my enduring thanks.

—Jose M. Fraguas

ABOUT THE AUTHOR

Born in Madrid, Spain, Jose M. Fraguas is regarded as one of the world's leading authorities and writers in the art of Karate-do. He began his Martial Arts training with judo, in grade school, at age 9 and studied Shito-ryu karate under Japanese master Masahiro Okada. Today, Fraguas still continues his "Karate-do path" under the guidance of Okada Sensei. He began his career as a writer at age 16 by serving as a regular contributor to Martial Arts magazines in Great Britain, France, Spain, Italy, Germany, Portugal, Holland, and Australia. A National Champion in Kata and Kumite, he was a member of the organization staff in the 5th W.U.K.O. (WKF) World Championships.

In 1980, he moved to Los Angeles, California, where his open-minded mentality helped him to develop a realistic approach to the Martial Arts. Seeking to supplement his previous training, he researched other disciplines under celebrated masters in order to better understand how other fighting methods apply the use of the human body in combat. Clearly, his physical training is always reflected in his works. "Spirit before technique. Feeling before writing. Writing should be a reflection of what you develop through training. I believe that Martial Arts are not just a practice or a lifestyle, but a mind-set and a tool to improve people's lives through their philosophy," Fraguas says.

In the mid-1980s, Fraguas founded his own book and magazine company, authoring dozens of books and distributing his magazines to 35 countries in five different languages. His reputation and credibility as a martial artist and publisher became well known to the top masters around the world. Considering himself a martial artist first and a writer and publisher second, Fraguas feels fortunate to have had the opportunity to interview many legendary Martial Arts teachers. He recognizes that much of the information given in the interviews helped him to discover new dimensions in the Martial Arts. "I was constantly absorbing knowledge from the great masters," he recalls. "I only had the opportunity to train physically with a few of them, but intellectually and spiritually, all of them have made very important contributions to my growth as a complete martial artist."

After authoring more than 27 books about Karate and Martial Arts, he worked to inspire others to follow, but only a few around thr world have successfully brought such drive and scholarship to their work. Fraguas has practiced, taught, and written about Karate-do for more than four decades. One of his works, the book series KARATE MASTERS – translated into several languages – has become a "classic" around the world and is considered as one of the best all-time sources of information about Karate's philosophy and knowledge.

In addition to his Karate-do training, Fraguas is a Motivational Speaker and Sports "Strength and Conditioning" training specialist. In that area, his focus is on the improvement of athletic capabilities through functional training systems. Working both with athletes in sports conditioning and non-athletes in more general conditioning, Fraguas has developed unique training programs that integrate proven methods with body-mind-spirit performance enhancement, as well as programs aimed specifically at Martial Arts performance.

He combines his personal experience, traditional Budo strategies and modern psychology to teach people how to act decisively, using cutting edge skills not only for physical training and sports but to effectively overcome any challenge in life.

He currently resides in Los Angeles, California.

INTRODUCTION

As part of Budo, karate-do is a way to understand the meaning of life (and death) from the warrior's perspective. It is correct to say that karate-do is supported by four pillars. In the first place, it can be understood as a life vision; second, as the proper spiritual way to realize this vision; third, as a set of physical techniques and specific tools for self-preservation; and finally, as a way to see Budo philosophy as the proper experience of freedom from death, which is its bigger objective. All these pillars act simultaneously to enhance our understanding of whom we truly are.

The true way of karate-do places a practitioner in a process of self-discovery. The process is one of continually freeing himself of concepts about who he is and of letting go of all the limitations imposed on his mind, so that he can know and fully express his essential nature. What the philosophy of karate-do means to each practitioner who truly understands its meaning simply cannot be defined; it is something everyone must discover for himself. Attaining self-knowledge is not like discovering the law of gravity. There is no benefit possible in the process of self-discovery except through personal effort. No matter how much one man drinks, he can't satisfy the thirst of another. All what he can do is recommend the process of drinking to those who are thirsty.

There are no shortcuts in the process of spiritual development. The practitioner has to develop as a whole, and, when only one of the aspects, such as the physical body, develops very quickly and the others are left behind, there are more obstacles and challenges in the medium and long run. Once a person awakens to his thirst for self-knowledge, his determination to succeed in life is reflected in the sincerity and strength of his search. Some like to talk about water but not look for it. Some like to discuss the available ways to search for water or hope that water will come to them out of the blue. Even some enjoy the process of looking for water so much that they avoid finding it. Only the sincere seeker feels keenly the thirst inside him and determines not to stop looking for water until the thirst is quenched.

The practice of karate in each country tends to reflect its cultural values. Some countries are more competitive and often karate training is used to alleviate the stress of the rapid pace of life. Westerners tend to work to conquer and perfect any project they undertake, including the practice of martial arts. This results in Westerner practitioners emphasizing the more external aspects of the art, such as the punching and kicking, while, at the same time, it makes it more difficult for them to understand the essence of Budo…with an attitude of balancing effort with surrender.

Any karate technique shown in this book falls into one of these two categories: sparring or self-defense. Those techniques developed to preserve the integrity of the practitioner in a self-defense situation won't work against a skilled opponent who knows how to move and counter any given attack. Techniques taken from the principles and concepts of traditional kata were not designed to be used under sportive environment or rules in which scoring a point is the main objective. On the other hand, those techniques that are sport oriented and were developed with the idea of obtaining a victory in a tournament are not advisable for a situation in which the self-preservation of the individual is at stake. The following techniques have been developed and perfected by world-class masters of karate. They have successfully been applied in competition and real combat. By using them, you can also enjoy success in your training, even if you are not a world-class competitor or karate practitioner. You must consistently practice each technique with a training partner, exploring all the possibilities of each movement, until you obtain the desired results based on your body type, athletic ability and physical attributes. Not all the techniques shown here will work for every practitioner. While karate basics are the same for everybody, the enjoyable part is that everyone can adapt and personalize them once the fundamental principles and concepts have been understood and physically absorbed.

When practiced under the guidance of a qualified instructor, and with the assistance of a willing training partner, the methods and techniques explained in this volume will be effective. They have been tested and proven for decades in the "laboratory" of practical experiences and the crucible of real competition.

Finally, regardless of what level the karate-do practitioner finds himself in, there is really only one teacher: experience itself. The true man of Budo follows one abiding principle: Pay attention to what is happening in his immediate experience. And this is something that cannot be expressed in words. As the famous Japanese writer Yukio Mishima, practitioner of karate-do and fifth dan in the art of kendo said, "Words are a medium that reduces reality to abstraction for transmission to our reason. In their power, they corrode reality. Inevitably, danger lurks that the words themselves will be corroded, too."

CONTENTS

173	195	213
VAL MIJAILOVIC	MINOBU MIKI	KUNIO MIYAKE
Gosoku-Ryu	*Shito-Ryu*	*Shito-Ryu*
229	241	249
TOM MUZILA	SEIJI NISHIMURA	EIHACHI OTA
Shotokan	*Wado-Ryu*	*Shorin-Ryu*
267	283	291
RICHARD RABAGO	AVI ROKAH	ALEX STERNBERG
Shorin-Ryu	*Shotokan*	*Shotokan*
301	325	331
KEIJI TOMIYAMA	TAMAS WEBER	KIYOSHI YAMAZAKI
Shito-Ryu	*Shito-Ryu*	*Ryobu-Kai*

PUTTING THE FIGHT BACK IN KATA

Patrick McCarthy

How many times have you learned a kata but had no idea what offensive themes its defensive principles actually addressed, or, that such themes even existed? It's a common problem that's been compared to learning a song in a foreign language. The song may be melodic, to be sure. However, if you can't speak the language, the meaning of the words remains a total mystery.

When you learn a kata without knowing about its inner workings, you might as well be dancing. Both holistic and anaerobic, kata is an important vehicle that helps you develop physical and mental qualities essential to karate-do. However, without first learning how to manipulate its defensive applications, kata alone is little more than physical exercise. By itself, kata does not teach the meaning of its techniques. Rather, it culminates defensive knowledge you already embrace, assuming you are fluent in every aspect of kata "language"—from techniques to applications.

Kata: The Time Capsule of Karate-do

Recognizing what kata represents is the first step to understanding the brutal usefulness locked within these remarkable geometric configurations. Those who understand the language with which kata is written will be rewarded handsomely because generations of defensive heritage are revealed. Developed by innovative Shaolin monks, kata embody practical defensive responses to habitual acts of physical violence through the use of open and empty hands. Historically guarded in an iron-clad ritual of secrecy, kata [*hsing* in Chinese] not only culminated a specific body of learning, it also served as the mnemonic vehicle through which the art has been passed down from one generation to the next.

Today, however, despite the widespread use of kata in virtually every style of martial arts instruction, its actual meaning has become obscured. There are two main reasons for this. First, many do not understand the nature of man the same way that the original Chinese pioneer masters did. Second, kata has been introduced and largely embraced as criteria for elevation from one rank to the next, as well as for display in today's rule-bound competitive arena of tournaments and expositions. Let's now look closer at the "anatomy" of kata.

Old School Kata

There are no unnecessary movements in the old school kata of orthodox karate. Every technique has a meaning and a purpose. However, recognizing this value first requires students to understand the fundamental premise and inner workings of kata. There are five sets of fundamental tools that make up the principal kata of old school karate. They are as follows:

1) Punches;
2) Kicks;
3) Stances;
4) Strikes;
5) Blocks…or parts thereof.

Classically, ritualized sets of associated exercises facilitated the development of these fundamental tools. These exercises included:

Various ways of punching with a closed fist;

A multitude of kicking techniques, leg maneuvers and corresponding techniques;

Drills that focused on mobility and posturing;

Open hand drills;

Associated methods of impact other than the fore-fist punch;

6) Finally, checking, trapping and blocking.

Historically speaking, delivery systems reflect an innovator's individual understanding and interpretation of these fundamental tools and are affectionately referred to as *ryuha* or *ryugi*. Despite the lip service paid to their omnipotence, ryuha represent nothing more nor less than individual teaching styles on defensive and/or competitive outcomes. It was karate pioneer Miyagi Chojun who deduced, in 1934, that "styles" are, "little more than teaching variations of common principles."

Defensive Principles

The fundamental defensive principles intertwined within kata were originally meant to include the following items:

1) Nerve stimulation;
2) Blood vessel obstruction;
3) Attacks on connective tissue structures (membrane, tendon, ligament and cartilage;
4) Joint locks and bone twists;
5) Takedowns;
6) Strangulation;

7) Throws;

8) Grappling;

9) Groundwork;

10) Counter attacks;

11) Attacks on other anatomically vulnerable zones such as the eyes, testicles, temples, etc.;

12) Attacks into the cavities of the body unprotected by the skeletal structure.

Historical Premise

The Shaolin monks also had some key kata principles. The monks believed that the human body was interrelated to itself and to nature. They concluded that anatomical and emotional conditions were influenced not only by our environment and diet, but also by specific physical stimulation. In TCM [traditional Chinese medicine], this concept is best explained by *qi* [chi], yin/yang and the 5 Element Theory. Through generations of empirical experience, these *quanfa* pioneers, within the confines of their monastic sanctuary, developed and gradually improved defensive applications based upon their understanding of this immutable knowledge.

As they continued to explore the principles of physical violence, energy transfer and the human body, these reclusive innovators developed an anatomical blueprint to exploit the synergy between any one part of the body and it's relation to the whole. Early learners understood that it was always the human body's unique function and common anatomical weaknesses that ultimately dictated how personal tools of impact, ways of seizing, and corresponding biomechanics of transferring both low intensity and higher velocity kinetic force best impeded motor performance, which is the dispassionate aim of self-defense.

After untold generations of continual study, a phenomenon for which the Shaolin order became well-known, innovative pioneers identified three distinct categories of physical violence that could be addressed with open and empty hands, as opposed to weapon attacks and responses. The first is mutual confrontation or anytime a defender is compelled to face an adversary and defend himself. Next, are habitual acts of physical violence. By virtue of the human body, there are only so many things that one person can do to another. For example, a headlock or a bearhug. Hence, these are habitual acts. Finally, there's clinching and struggling. This is what usually happens in between mutual confrontations, especially if or when the initial attack or defense is unsuccessful. A clinch and a struggle, either standing or on the ground, is often what occurs before a "habitual act" can be achieved.

The Shaolin monks went on to identify and catalogue no less than 36 habitual acts of physical violence that plagued their plebeian society. Moreover, as they continued to improve their skills, as many as 72 variations on these offensive scenarios were further identified, which in turn gave birth to a plethora of unique training drills. Ultimately, this knowledge became a systematized methodology, known as

Shaolin quanfa [*kenpo* in Japanese]: i.e. The laws of using one's fist.

Two-Man Drills

The most successful way in which early Shaolin innovators could repeatedly bring students into direct contact with each act of physical violence—without the threat of serious injury—was to recreate the acts in a safe learning environment. They did this so they could explore defensive parameters and negotiate human error, while simultaneously acquiring skills and experience. By actually recreating individual acts of physical violence in ritualized movement, learners were able to work with varying partners [big, small, strong, weak, et cetera] at their own pace and gain valuable experience. In turn, this experience provided the foundation for further study of the overall nature of physical violence and the opportunity to continually improve defensive practices.

Described in flowery ways [*Dragon Spits Pearls, Wind Whistles Around the Tree, Catching a Flapping Fish,* et cetera], Shaolin quanfa pioneers incrementally developed 18 hsing/kata to culminate the 108 ritualized two-man training drills that linked offensive scenarios to corresponding defensive principles. Of these 18 solo signature rituals, six specialized in striking anatomically vulnerable zones with the fists; two specialized in using the palms; one used the elbows, shoulders, head, and knees; four utilized foot and leg maneuvers; and five specialized in grappling.

Tatakawa Zuishite Katsu—Victory Without Contention

Peaceful by nature and resolved to living life in harmony with nature and their fellow man, Shaolin monks reasoned that by learning to control their emotions and ego the need for physical violence could be reduced to pure chance…the chance that someone actually seized hold of them. Even then, the mandate was to restrain or control the attacker…never to brutalize anyone. An old Shaolin principle states, "Avoid fighting at all cost. However, when no other choice is available, restrain rather than fight and hurt rather than kill, for all life is precious and none can ever be replaced."

Martial arts history is filled with gallant tales of Shaolin monks and Daoist priests avoiding physical violence by turning the other cheek and walking—if not running away—from ego-related confrontations. When this phenomenon is deeply studied, it becomes apparent that all too often our human condition (ego) is responsible for so many of today's unnecessary violent street encounters. Our inability to control our ego and emotions has long been considered the catalyst for acts of physical violence. Hence, the study of karate-do has always emphasized a body of moral philosophy with which to govern the behavior of learners who embrace its brutal practice.

Kata: Mnemonic Rituals

Of the 50 or so old school kata collected and handed down from Okinawa's old Ryukyu Kingdom, rarely did any master embrace more than one or two kata in his overall training curriculum. That is because local masters of that era successfully imparted their delivery system through the two-man training drills that connected offensive scenarios to corresponding defensive application principles. The resulting composite techniques and signature solo practices evolved into kata.

Master teachers focused upon actual applications rather than how "good" the kata looked! The key was function…not form. Although it's hard to accept today—especially during a time when kata is practiced more for physical development, holistic value, competitive purpose or advancement in rank—kata, as originally learned in old school karate, culminated the defensive lessons students had already been taught.

Moreover, students of the same school did not always learn things the same way. Classical instruction was most often conducted on a one-on-one basis, with an eye toward the student's age and abilities, etc. Teaching techniques also varied with the master's age and experience. Thus, the teaching methods he employed as an adult varied from those of his youth. This is especially true when the more holistic, inward and softer aspects of the art became more appealing. Group classes, like we see today, only became popular because Itosu Ankoh revolutionized the tradition.

This, by the way, is the man regarded by many as the grandfather of modern karate.

Itosu Ankoh (1832–1915) collected and standardized the practice of many kata into a single tradition around the turn of the 20th Century. Based upon this analysis, he went on to develop shorter geometrical representations of the older and longer traditions, which he called the *pinan/heian* kata. Up until that time in Okinawa's three principal districts (the old castle capital of Shuri, Kumemura, the Chinese district of Naha and the deep water port of Tomari), there were about 50 or so old school kata that Itosu sensei and his colleague, Higashionna Kanryo (1853-1917), brought together to establish specific schools, including *chinto (gankaku), chinte, happoren (paipuren), hakutsuru, jiin, jion, jitte, kururunfua, kushankun (kanku dai/sho), naifanchin (tekki), nanshu, nepai (nipaipo), passai (bassai dai/sho), rohai (meikyo), rakkaken, sobarinpai (peichurrin), sanseru, seipai, seiunchin, seisan (hangetsu), shisoochin, sochin, unshu (unsu), useishi (gojushiho sho/dai), wando (wanduan), wankan (matsukaze)* and *wanshu (enpi).*

Built upon ancient customs, profound spiritual conviction and disciplined social ideology, it is important to remember that the kata of karate-do, and the way they are embraced now during modern times, mirror the Japanese culture from whence they came. This is true, despite the cultural context of their Chinese origins and the fact that the Chinese-based Okinawan culture vigorously embraced them long before being introduced to the mainland of Japan at the dawn of the 20th century. We should also bear in mind that kata is the only reason karate-do, as a ritualized tradition, still exists today. This art is as much a product of our lives as our lives are a product of the art.

Non-Defensive Benefits of Kata

Kata does more than address the habitual acts of physical violence that plague society. It also represents a profound holistic and therapeutic application. On the surface, kata training strengthens bone and muscle, which helps maximize your biomechanics. This refers to developing optimum performance and includes the ability to vibrate, torque and rotate your hips, and expand and contract your muscles. This is the total summation of joint forces. Kata also improves concentration and the functions of various organs in the body. The controlled breathing techniques, vigorous twisting of the body, oscillation of the limbs, and the contraction and expansion of the muscles not only opens up *jingluo*, blood and the lymphatic vessels, it improves the functions of the skeleton and muscular structures and the digestive system.

Your ability to build, contain and release energy is enhanced through your ability to regulate your breathing and synchronize it with the expansion and contraction of muscle activity. Air is the gateway between the mental and physical and one principal concern in the practice of kata. Because of this element, kata is also an excellent source of oxygenating the body and cultivating *Ki* energy that has an incredibly positive therapeutic effect upon the body. In light of this deeper knowledge, you can see why kata is such an excellent way to keep the body electrically charged and physically tuned.

Finally, kata can be a provocative alternative in stress management. Such a practice not only increases your ability to respond effectively to potentially dangerous encounters, it also empowers you to better deal with the enormous levels of stress encountered in daily life. Learning how to respond dispassionately to unwarranted aggression requires self-empowerment. In short, kata serves to develop this attribute, along with a healthy body, fast reflexes and strong movements.

Problems of Today

At the forefront of today's highly divided international karate community, there are a growing number of concerned instructors who are anxious to better understand kata in its entirety. Sadly, this issue has given rise to unprecedented eclecticism…rather than promoting an inward exploration of kata itself. Instructors making the transition from the competitive element to old school learning remain locked in a classical paradox. Perplexed by differences that separate competitive athleticism from civil self-defense, the real question surrounds how to make functional sense out of ritualized technique, what to hold on to and what to discard.

23

Traveling and teaching kata throughout the world over the past few years, I must concur with my American colleague David Lowry, who in his publication *Sword & Brush* wrote, "Those lacking a firsthand acquaintance with them (kata) are unlikely to take such a respectful view of classical kata. They usually interpret them to be a sterile, mindlessly repetitive imitation with little relevance to real fighting. For those not involved intimately with them, the appearance of kata is of choreographed dance with rigidly set patterns devoid of any spontaneity."

It is only from an informed and inside perspective that you can begin to grasp the enormous and widespread benefit kata contains. Kata is truly a metaphor, as what you see on the outside is never what lies within its package. What may appear on the surface to be robotic and impractical is actually a brilliant method of instruction, which, with adequate guidance, allows a learner to achieve unfettered outcomes. Because the body has changed little in the years since kata was developed, it would make sense that the corresponding application principles intertwined in these ancient ritualized forms are as effective today as they were in the beginning.

Flowing Peacefulness

Beyond exhaustion and despite aching muscles, you [and most everyone] have experienced a peacefulness flowing quietly within the brutality of your kata training.

Indeed, it is through this inner-tranquility that your pursuit of spiritual harmony is realized. By adhering to the Shaolin precepts upon which of karate-do unfolded (Step-by-step improvement; constant learning and practice; temperance in all things; peacefulness of mind; and honor the virtues of courtesy and respect) you come face to face with your weaknesses. Through these teachings, weaknesses are turned into strengths and strengths into even greater strengths. Throughout the ages, masters of karate have always maintained that this tradition conditions the body, cultivates the mind and nurtures the spirit, compelling each learner to contribute to the welfare of humanity. Hence, the tradition fulfills its purpose. The source of human weakness is internal, not external. Discovering where the source of human weakness lies reveals the inner location in which all of our battles should be first fought and won before the art of karate can ever serve to improve the living of our daily lives. This message is far more important than the physical conduit through which it is achieved.

As you perfect yourself through the study of this remarkable tradition, you are reminded to never again forget or remove the fight from within the kata. Not only is it the very source from which the art was cradled, but from it evolves the inherent lesson teaching us to respect, preserve and cherish life. As the wisdom of Funakoshi Gichin reveals: "The ultimate aim of karate lies not in victory nor defeat but in the perfection of the character of its participants."

REACTIONS IN KARATE

Avi Rokah

Reactions in karate are based on feeling, action and technique. These are the elements that comprise reactions or dictate just how fast you move. If your reactions are fast, reaction and action blend into one without any delay. To be truly fast, you have to "feel" what's going on and react. This is much faster than a conscious reaction, which takes time.

If someone attacked you on the street, you initially would be surprised. Next, you'd analyze the situation and make a decision. An "order" is subsequently sent from the brain to the nervous system. Nerve impulses "race" from the outgoing nervous system to the muscle ends and then you execute the technique. To be faster, you want to reduce the time of analyzation and decision-making. You want to react before you have to analyze what is happening in your conscious brain. You want the process to go directly from the nervous system to body action (rotation, vibration, shitting, et cetera) to the technique.

Of course, your body action depends on the technique direction and distance. With enough repetition training in many circumstances, your body will know what to do, you'll execute properly and the technique will happen. This whole process should be ingrained in your system. That's why *jiyu-kumite* is important. When you properly master basic techniques, you learn to move efficiently and create proper patterns in the nervous system. Therefore, when something happens, such as an attack, you react from the nervous system in the spine, through body action and technique. If you practice incorrectly and move your arms and legs independently, you will suffer several problems. First, the technique will be weak. Second, there will always be a conscious decision first and then movement. This takes time, and that can be a problem because the difference between winning and losing can be hundredths of a second.

To eliminate that potential problem, you can do repetition of basic techniques. With enough of this type of training, nerve impulses will travel faster to the muscle ends. Compare this to an old, rusty hose (an untrained person). At first, the water doesn't flow smoothly. However, after using the hose a few times, the water will go through smoother (a trained person). Nishiyama Sensei said that there are three

things important in the martial arts (eyes, feet and guts). Whatever the eyes see, he said, the feet should react simultaneously. And guts, or strong spirit, allow the feet to "express" the eyes without hesitation or doubt.

Following are some guidelines to react without conscious thought or interference from the mind.

The Eyes

The actual eyes should look "soft" or calm, but the "feeling" should be strong. You need to look at your opponent, but you can't focus intently on one area. You need to keep a broader focus. Use your peripheral vision. In essence, you should look spontaneously and without intention. The *kami tanden*, which is a space located between the eyes, is the upper center of energy. (This is a branch of the lower tanden that is located under the navel). The upper tanden "shoots" *Ki* or mental energy to the opponent. If you look strongly with your eyes, you will receive too much information. In essence, you'll be trying to watch everything, and you can't function that way. This, in turn, brings doubt, and you'll be one step behind your opponent.

Direction To Your Technique

From the lower tanden, or the lower center of energy, Ki, or mental energy, is already "shooting" at your opponent. And, every part of your body also projects to this direction. In essence—mentally—your technique has already hit the opponent. You might say that the engine is already running. If you don't have that direction established, your technique will always be late. In this case, you will have to make a decision and then move. More importantly, the natural reflex of human beings is to cover the head and throat when attacked. However, you cannot afford to cover and then counterattack. That is why it's imperative that you establish mental direction and that your kamae arms are directed to the opponent's center. This will help develop the spirit of *ai-uchi* or mutual killing. Now, this doesn't mean that you will always react with an attack. What it does mean, however, is that if you block, attack, shift out of the way and attack [*go-no-sen*], you are always on the way to the opponent. And a block, by the way, is an attack. There is no block and then attack; it's one line of energy.

It is also important to distinguish between giving direction to your technique and giving an order. Giving an order makes you fixed-minded. If you give an order to one arm or the other, it will take time to shift your mind [to the next move] if another technique is necessary. Giving direction means that any technique can be released from your center at any time. In this case, the mind is distributed correctly.

Firm, Elastic Center

The center of your body should be firm and "elastic." However, it should not be too stiff or too relaxed. It's difficult to quantify this exactly, because there is no way to measure how much tension or relaxation you should have. It might be best to think in terms of a cat chasing a rat. It can't be too relaxed or too stiff. If it's one extreme or the other, it won't be able to chase the rat fluidly. You can also think of a mad, dangerous dog. Think of how he prepares himself internally and the sound that he emits when he's in attack mode. So, the center of your body should be like a spring ready to explode. It should have potential energy, without external change. Technically, you should keep your tailbone in, your lower stomach firm, you should "shoot" forward and you should push your navel slightly back. This will stabilize your lower back and allow you to initiate a technique using the back muscles. Restrict your breath to your lower abdominals so you can always use muscle reaction by exerting pressure to the ground.

Breath, Sound, Kiai Reaction

The unconscious, primitive area of the brain is known as the medulla. Underneath this sits the breathing control center. When something happens, the reflex is initially a sound. This occurs before you even realize what has happened. This type of situation or reflex is also used in karate when you *Kiai*. When you shout a Kiai, this will help you bypass your conscious brain. Your Kiai should "hit" your opponent and your technique follows.

As described in the previous article *(Stages of Technique)*, the sequence of throwing a proper technique is as follows: Ki, Kiai and then the technique. Your breathing initiates your muscle action and technique, so proper basics and proficiency in kata give you the tools for good reactions. Make sure that you don't start with a muscular reaction and then breathe, because this will make you stiff and slow before you even move. It's also important to make sure that your

breath does not rise to your chest because this can make you become anxious and unstable. In this scenario, the technique starts with the shoulders and arms.

Remember, do not include your mind in the technique. You don't want to employ a logical process of thinking here. Naturally, you will ask, "Doesn't karate teach us not to think? Aren't we supposed to be like an animal?" On the contrary, the one with the better mind will win. To be sure, that is contingent on how natural your reaction is and if you can trust your ability to respond to any attack. If so, your mind is free for strategy. If you are unsure about yourself, you will always be over protective, unstable emotionally and unable to take risks. When you are confident and calm, you can use your intelligence best.

There are a variety of training drills and tips that will enhance reactions. Let's look at them now.

Timing and Application of Oji Waza *(Go No Sen)*

Oji waza [responding techniques] are most important in your kumite training. Even if you don't know how to attack or set-up, oji waza can still be used successfully in a self-defense situation if you are confident in your ability to respond to any attack. On the other hand, you won't be able to set up and respond to the chance that you create if you are not able to respond to any attack. You might say that a good offense depends on a good defense.

Amashi Waza

Amashi waza is a technique in which you use space to avoid a first attack and counter before a second technique. As with *sen* [early timing], the reaction in amashi waza coincides with your breathing [exhale]. And you should exhale toward yourself, as if pulling the opponent to you. You don't want to exhale in an outward direction. Your breathing also has to be synchronized with your feet. When your breathing starts, move your feet back—neither fast nor slow—at the same rhythm of the attack. You shouldn't move back too far or too little. Just let the opponent touch your skin. Normally, one inch of shifting is enough. When sliding back, keep your lower stomach [tanden] close to the opponent, so your pelvis doesn't tilt backwards. If you tilt your pelvis backwards, you will have to spend more time shifting forward to counterattack, and you will not be able to create pressure on the ground to launch an effective counterattack.

When moving back, no power is necessary. Moving backward is simply your preparation for a counterattack. During this process, the key is how quickly you switch from moving back to moving forward. Use your breathing to create the shortest, sharpest pressure to the ground. It's almost like a bouncing ball or a spring. If you stop or go too far back, your opponent can continue his attack. Switch sharply from exhaling toward yourself to exhaling outwards to the opponent. The switch should be just before the opponent completes his attack or about the last 10 percent of his action. A good indicator will be that your back foot touches the ground just before the opponent's advancing foot touches the ground. Thus, going back is being in tune with the opponent's rhythm. Changing direction to counterattack will break the rhythm.

One Step

As an initial step of training for this, learn to estimate the opponent's attacking distance for various techniques and distances. In call cases, you want to slide back so he just touches your skin. Remember, while your opponent has to cover all the space [distance] between the two of you, [1 or 2 feet, for example], you only have to move back 1 or 2 inches. Your feet make the main adjustments of space, but you can make additional small adjustments by leaning your head away from him. So, you don't have to be nearly as fast as your opponent, but your timing has to be good.

As you might have guessed, there are some problems that may develop. For example, if you look and then move, this gives a good fighter enough time to catch you. Therefore, you don't want to use your eyes to react. Instead, you want to use your breathing to catch the opponent's rhythm...then you should react. Using your eyes means waiting, analyzing, making a decision and then moving. Train yourself to catch the opponent's rhythm with your breath before he moves. And, of course, you always have to be ready for your Kiai.

When the opponent attacks with a kick and you move straight back, the range of the kick might allow space for his next attack before you can counter. In this case, you "catch" the opponent's rhythm before executing your counterattack. While you catch the rhythm, you use a side-shift or *kawashi* [switching the hips out of the line of attack] to avoid the opponent's line of attack. In the meantime, position yourself in the best counterattacking position.

Usually, against a back-leg kick, it's prudent to employ a side-shift. If your left leg is forward, move your right foot to the right. Your left foot follows in a crescent action toward the right foot and the opponent. Note, don't shift your weight onto your right foot. However, you should create pressure on your right foot. While doing this, your center should move minimally. There are for two reasons for this. First, if you shift too much, your opponent will follow with another technique. Two, if you shift your weight to the right foot, you can't use the ground for support when you throw your counterattack, because the angle between your right foot and the center of your body becomes too big. When your right foot touches the floor, the angle of your foot and knee should be toward the opponent. As a reminder, you are always on the way to the opponent, even if you go sideways in between. You want to place your right foot in the best space for your counterattack.

Against a front leg kick? It's best to use kawashi, which means you switch your hips out of the line of attack without moving the center of your body. This is the method of choice because it's fast. If the opponent kicks with his front leg, react and "catch" his rhythm with your breathing and feet. Exhale towards yourself, switch the axis of your body, and push your left knee, hip and shoulder toward the opponent. Keep your lower left leg firm, while you move your back foot in a small circle to the left. Remember, there is no weight on the back foot. When your right foot touches the floor, breathe sharply and change direction so you can counterattack.

You should throw your counterattack when the opponent extends his kicking leg. When the foot passes your body, change rhythm and counterattack. In both side-shifting and *kawashi,* pay attention to keep your weight steady. This is difficult, but you have to be able to suspend and control the leg from the center of your body. The muscles of the backside are of particular importance; make sure your buttocks stay firm and your lower stomach is close to the opponent. Your eyes should be diverted from your opponent. Otherwise, your legs will become heavy and will move independently from the body.

In all three cases (back-shifting, sideshifting or *kawashi),* the first part of the movement—avoiding and riding on the opponent's attack—is not independent from the counterattack. It's preparation for the counterattack, so you can accumulate energy for the counter. Look at it as one action, even though sometimes you can practice the first half separately to check that you don't over shift, don't lose your center and that you are in tune to the opponent's timing, space and line of attack.

Let's now look at *kake-no-sen* and *zanshin,* which is the essence of oji waza.

Kake-no-sen

Catching the Opponent During His Intention to Move

In this exercise, two partners face each other. The one who attacks will execute a surprise charge and throw a half technique. For example, your partner can move forward with a feeling and intention of a real attack. However, he should only bend his arm or leg halfway. And, he should not charge with a pattern routine; otherwise, this becomes just an aerobic exercise without reaction. Your goal (the responding side) is to anticipate and catch him as early as possible. If you see him move, you are too late. You should see him before he completes his shifting. Following are some tips that should help you.

Preparation

Mikiru—Estimate the opponent's distance and potential movement.

Eyes—Look softly. Don't concentrate on one area. Act as if you are looking from a distance, as this gives you an overview. This is like an overview. In between your eyes, [the upper tanden] establish a strong shooting feeling.

Give direction to your technique. From your lower stomach, [tanden] "shoot" Ki (mental energy) through the opponent. Your grip should be firm. If your hands are open, maintain a strong feeling at the top of your hands. This is especially important for your little fingers and underneath your arms. A firm grip allows connection to the elbows and permits energy to extend through the arms to the opponent. Remember, keep your elbows and shoulders soft.

Body condition—Your center of gravity should be forward, your front foot should be light, your stomach pressing back, your back firm and you should be ready to exhale or Kiai. It's hard to say how tense or relaxed the center of your body should be. It's a matter of experience. Think of an animal ready to jump on its prey. You should not be too tense or too relaxed. Wind up internally. Don't use your eyes to follow and react to the opponent. Use your breathing to adjust to the opponent's rhythm and react. Using your eyes causes hesitation and disorganized reaction. Remember, the decision is already made. Your mental energy already passes through the opponent; thus, use your breathing to adjust to the rhythm and to react. Your muscles and technique will follow.

Ho Shin—Give yourself away. Once you move, give everything. Don't worry about winning or losing. Your body center should hit the opponent.

Budo Principle—This entails the following: a) eyes; b) feet; c) guts (spirit); d) power (technique). This means that whatever your eyes see, you should express through your feet...without interference from your brain. Guts/spirit mean that there should be no hesitation. Once you move, don't hold back until you have finished. e) keep your target away from the opponent, and keep your weapon close to the opponent. So, that means keep your eyes and face away from the opponent, and keep your lower stomach and fists close to him. Make your territory big. Also, when your center of gravity is close to the opponent, it has to travel less when you shift. Remember, don't wait because that puts you behind his rhythm and on the defensive. Instead, you should feel as if you are chasing your opponent. You dictate the rhythm. In any case, when delivering your technique, your body action and breathing are first. Technique follows, and the proper timing is critical. When excited, the tendency is to move your arms before—and independently—from your body. You should be able to accomplish this if you do this drill with *tsuki-waza* (punching) and *keri-waza* (kicking).

Next, do the same drill but change things up a bit. This time the one who charges should move around front, back or laterally and then execute a surprise charge. And there is one more important element to consider. *Ukimi* means floating. In essence, you would use the center of your body (abdominals, glutes, groin and inner thigh muscles) to suspend your legs. Imagine, for example, that the outside of your legs are a tube and the inside of your legs are suspended. You should feel as if you are walking on air. Of course, your feet are touching the floor, but you don't put any weight or pressure on your feet. This means that the joints are free and

at any moment you could apply pressure to floor to initiate a technique. And don't forget...while moving, keep your elbows connected, your breathing rhythmic and be ready to Kiai.

Sen (timing) Plus Zanshin (mental awareness)

Do this drill stationary the first time. In subsequent drills, the one who attacks should move or charge with a half tech-

nique. As soon as the responding side finishes his technique, the partner should again charge a second and third time with a half technique. The responding side anticipates with *sen* timing—two or three times if necessary—while adapting to the changing distance. The idea is to eliminate all space between kime to kime [*kamae*]. Following are some important points.

• The first entails Kiai. When reacting to each of your opponent's moves, don't stop breathing and don't inhale between each Kiai. When one Kiai ends, the next one should already be starting. If you don't do that, you're creating a space or a chance for your opponent to react. Moreover, once you inhale, you start using slow muscle fibers. Besides, within one combination that only takes a few seconds, there is no need to inhale.

• During each kime, exert pressure downward. It's like putting the brake on while still pushing the accelerator. Release the brake and your next technique starts. Thus, your Kiai changes direction, but the momentum doesn't stop and restart. You might even compare this to a railroad. The line of energy or the momentum is already set. Your first and second techniques ride on the same railroad. Don't use your eyes between techniques and don't recalculate or you will be behind. Don't wait. Attack your opponent's action. Invite his attack as if telling him, "Come, come."

• *Ho-shin* means you give yourself away. So, give everything you've got in the first technique; destroy the opponent with that first technique. Don't do the first technique while thinking of getting ready for the next. The best way to be ready for the next technique is to put everything into the first. The more momentum and pressure you develop during kime, the more naturally and powerfully the following technique starts. Also, by giving yourself away mentally (having *no-mind* in the technique), your mind will be full for the next technique; you will have no holdbacks or hesitations.

How To Avoid Mistakes

The moment you hit your opponent you don't want to lose this advantage by making any mistakes. Following are a few things to avoid:

• *Snap-back*

When you snap-back, you stop your momentum and this creates an opportunity for the opponent to recover. Plus, the momentum from the technique is not fully delivered through the opponent. So, when you snap-back, it's like going to a reverse gear. Avoid this.

• *Stop the Opponent's Next Action*

You can stop one of the opponent's moves, but you have to be cautious of his follow-up techniques. If you give him space to come back, you will lose your momentum. So, your best defense is to attack and anticipate your opponent's actions.

• *Cover Yourself After an Attack*

If you're guilty of this, you will give your opponent a chance for another attack. Granted, you can cover one area, but a good opponent will find open space. How do you prevent this? Once you hit your opponent, don't give him a chance until you destroy him.

YOSHIAKI AJARI

WADO-RYU

Yoshiaki Ajari began training in the goju-ryu style of karate-do under Shozo Ujita sensei. He eventually became a direct student of the founder of wado-ryu karate, Hironori Otsuka, when he went to Meiji University to further his studies. Yoshiaki Ajari is one of the leading teachers of the style around the world and an active member of the World Karate Federation. As a chief instructor of the U.S. Wado Kai, he travels extensively to spread the "art of peace," as the founder advised. His restless spirit and inquiring mind have made him very critical of those who do not teach the art in the proper and traditional way.

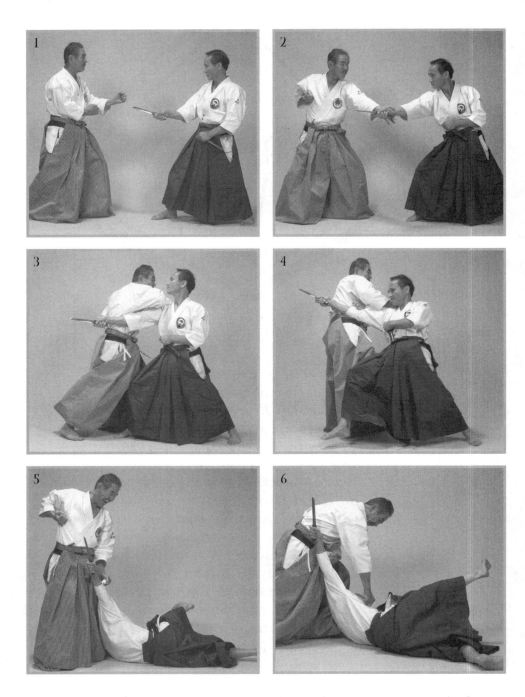

Ajari Sensei facing his armed opponent (1). As the aggressor initiates the front attack, Ajari side-steps to the left and deflects the arm with his left hand (2), following with a elbow attack to the face (3), and a sweep to the opponent's right leg (4), which brings him to the ground (5), where Ajari finishes off with a punch (6).

Ajari squares off with his opponent (1). The opponent attacks with a direct punch to the face and Ajari deflects it with his right arm (2). As soon as the opponent follows up with a new punch, Ajari Sensei uses his right elbow to block the attack (3), followed by a downward punch to the groin (4). Then, he grabs the opponent's right leg (5), and brings him to the ground (6), where he punches him in the groin (7).

Ajari faces his opponent, who is armed with a sword (1). As soon as the opponent steps in with the attack, Ajari sidesteps and hits the opponent's throat with his left hand (2), following with a side kick to the knee (3), and a counter-attack with haito-uchi to the face (4-5).

Ajari faces his opponent (1). When the opponent attacks with his left hand, Ajari Sensei uses the outside of his forearm to deflect the incoming punch (2), and uses the same hand to block the attacker's second punch (3). Immediately, he controls the attacking hand with his left hand and applies an upward elbow counter to the opponent's chin (4).

43

TINO CEBERANO

GOJU-RYU

After receiving his third-dan certificate from the legendary Gogen "The Cat" Yamaguchi, a young Tino Ceberano left his native country of Hawaii to establish the style of goju-ryu karate in Melbourne, Australia. From small beginnings, this style of karate has grown and multiplied, becoming the most widely practiced of karate styles in Australia. His fighting approach, based on effectiveness and practicality, soon gained numerous followers and brought him recognition as one of the most effective karate teachers around the world.

Ceberano Sensei faces his opponent (1). As soon as the opponent steps in to attack with a reverse punch, Ceberano slightly steps back to create distance (2), controls the attacking arm (3), and applies a jodan ura-mawashi geri to the opponent's face (4).

Ceberano Sensei is grabbing from the back (1). He lifts both arms to break the grip (2), and immediately hits the opponent with a backward elbow to the chest (3) and a tetsui-uchi to the groin (4).

47

Ceberano Sensei squares off against his opponent (1). Ceberano initiates the attack by closing the gap using a front kick, that is deflected by his opponent (2). Immediately, he throws a jodan tsuki to the face that is blocked (3), and a chudan tsuki that is intercepted by the opponent (4). Using his left hand, Ceberano Sensei tries to hit the stomach but the strike is blocked (5). Maintaining contact with his opponent's arm, Ceberano grabs the wrist and hits, with his left arm, the opponent's elbow (6), following with an outside sweep (7) and a final shuto-uchi to the throat (8).

Ceberano faces his opponent (1). The opponent attacks with a reverse punch that is blocked by Ceberano Sensei (2), as is his second attempt to hit with the left hand (3). Ceberano then strikes with a finger jab to the eyes (4), strikes the opponent's left elbow (5), and finishes him off with a shuto-uchi to the face as he unbalances him with a leg strike to the back of the left leg (6).

49

Ceberano faces his opponent (1). The opponent initiates the offensive attacking with a front kick that is deflected by Ceberano Sensei using sukui-uke (2). Then, Ceberano controls the attacking leg and opponent's right arm, and closes the distance (3) to apply a final sweep (4).

Ceberano Sensei squares off with his opponent (1). The opponent initiates the attack with a left punch (2) that Ceberano deflects with his left hand after using a check with his right (3). Immediately, he controls the attacking arm and lifts his left knee (4) to apply a mawashi-geri chudan that is blocked by the opponent (5), and followed by a reverse punch to the face that hits the target (6).

51

Ceberano Sensei faces his opponent (1). The aggressor steps in and grabs Ceberano by the neck (2), to which Sensei reacts by using his left hand to secure the grip (3), and attacking the opponent's throat (4), as he simultaneously applies a wrist lock (5).

Ceberano Sensei faces his opponent (1). As soon as the opponent steps in, Ceberano Sensei uses his right hand to cover his opponent's vision (2), and strikes with a front kick to the groin (3), followed by an upward elbow to the chin (4), and an armlock (5) that brings the opponent to the ground (6).

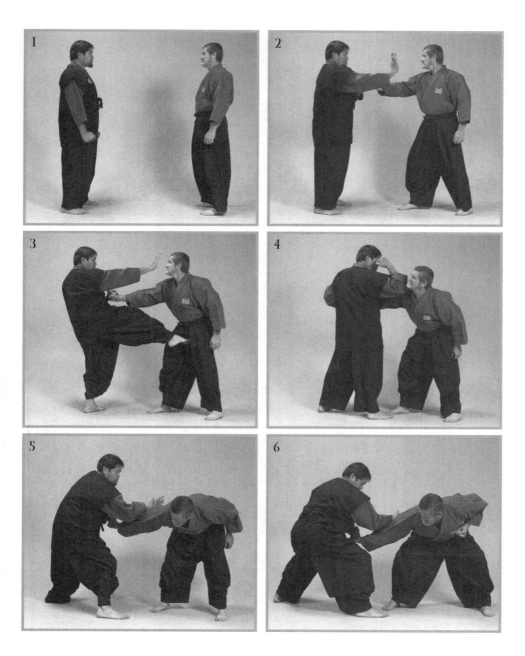

53

Ceberano Sensei faces his opponent (1). As soon as the opponent grabs his lapels, Ceberano Sensei hits the opponent's face with a palm strike (2), followed by an elbow strike (3), and a shoulder lock in combination of a shuto-uchi to the back of the neck (4).

The opponent grabs Ceberano Sensei's right wrist (1). Sensei uses a clockwise motion of his right hand and simultaneously secures the opponent's grabbing hand with his left (2) to immediately apply pressure and deliver a front kick to the stomach (3) that finishes his opponent off (4).

55

Ceberano Sensei squares off against his opponent (1). As soon as the opponent initiates the front kick, Ceberano Sensei sidesteps (2) and grabs the kicking leg with his right arm, as he simultaneously controls the opponent's right arm (3) to throw him off balance and onto the ground (4).

Ceberano Sensei is facing his opponent (1). The opponent attacks with a straight punch to the face that is deflected by Ceberano's right hand (2). Sensei Ceberano immediately counterattacks with a roundhouse kick to the groin (3), and applies a final armbar to control the opponent (4).

Ceberano Sensei squares off against his opponent (1). With his left hand, he parries the first of the opponent's attack and (2) uses the same hand to block the second punch (3), followed by a counter punch to the face and (4) a right elbow (5). Then he uses his right hand to control the opponent's neck (6) and finishes with an upward knee to the chest (7).

Ceberano faces his aggressor (1). As soon as the aggressor grabs Ceberano's neck (2), Sensei uses both hands to break the grip (3) and immediately attacks with a palm strike to the face (4), followed by an elbow strike (5) and a knee to the lower back (6).

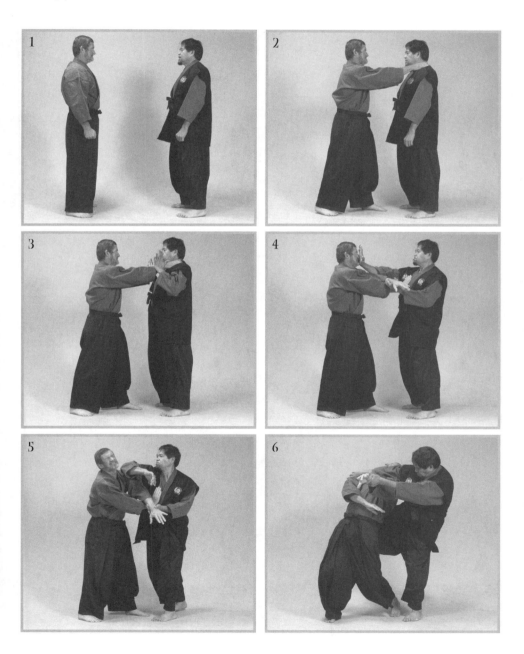

RAY DALKE

SHOTOKAN

Known for never pulling any punches—either in or out of the dojo—Sensei Dalke is a true icon of a bygone era in which students were allowed to spar and train with the best masters in the world. Shoulder-to-shoulder with such names as Kanzawa, Enoeda and Shirai, Ray Dalke forged his technique and spirit under the demanding attention of JKA great, Hidetaka Nishiyama. After more than four decades of up and downs in the way of Budo, Dalke keeps walking the same path, immersing himself in the practice and development of his beloved art, with no changes in his mind about what karate is or is not.

Sensei Dalke faces his opponent (1). Using his right hand to cover the angle, he enters (2) and applies a sweeps to the opponent's left leg (3), followed by a gyaku-tsuki jodan (4). He then sweeps with his left leg (5), bringing his opponent down to the ground (6), where he finishes him with a punch to the chest (7).

Sensei Dalke squares off against his opponent (1). His opponent tries to sweeps Dalke's left leg, but he avoids it by retracting his foot (2). Using this to get attack momentum (3), he applies a mae-mawashi-geri chudan (4) to his opponent's stomach (5) and spins into a tetsui-uchi (6-7). Pivoting over himself, he delivers a sweep to his opponent's right leg, bringing him down to the ground (8), where he finishes him with a straight punch (9).

空手術

63

Dalke Sensei faces his opponent (1). When the aggressor attacks with oi-tsuki, Dalke reacts by ducking under the attack and delivering a gyaku-tsuki chudan (2), but still controls the attacking arm (3). He then grabs the opponent's right leg (4), takes him to the ground (5), and finishes him with a punch to the face (6).

Dalke Sensei squares off against his opponent (1), who attacks with a left hand punch to the face, which Dalke sidesteps (2). Dalke follows with a side kick to the face (3-4), and an inside sweep to the opponent's left leg (5), which unbalances and takes him to the ground (6), where Dalke finishes him with a punch to the head (7).

FUMIO DEMURA

SHITO-RYU

He is a superb technician, a great martial artist, and one of the finest performers and weapons experts in the world. He is credited with being the first professional karate performer to incorporate lights, music, costumes and martial arts into the same routine. His technical prowess is breathtaking—as is the trademark precision of his punches and kicks. Easy-going and affable, he is one of the most accessible karate masters from which to learn. Fumio Demura is the type of person that people naturally follow as a leader.

Demura Sensei faces his opponent (1). He moves in, initiating mae-tsuki with the right hand over the opponent's left arm, to have a superior positioning (2). At the moment of impact, Demura's left hand checks the opponent's lead arm for better control (3).

Demura Sensei squares off against his opponent (1). As soon as the opponent initiates the attack with a reverse punch, Demura sidesteps to the left (2) and finalizes the counter with a gyaku-tsuki to the body (3).

Demura faces his opponent on uneven lead (1). The opponent attacks with a reverse punch, to which Demura reacts by side-stepping to the right (2), and blocking with his left hand, using gedan-barai (3). Immediately, he turns his body to the right (4), and applies a reverse punch to the face (5).

Demura Sensei and his opponent face each other (1). When the opponent attacks with a reverse punch, Demura Sensei sidesteps to the left (2), blocks with his left hand (3), and immediately counters with a ura-ken to the face (4).

Demura Sensei squares off against his opponent (1). The opponent attacks with a mae-geri chudan that Demura blocks with his left hand and simultaneously steps back to create distance (2). When the opponent puts his attacking leg on the floor, Demura Sensei moves in (3) and applies a final shuto-uchi to the face (4).

Demura Sensei squares off against his opponent (1). The opponent attacks with a mae-geri chudan that Demura blocks with his left hand and simultaneously steps back to create distance (2). This time, Demura counterattacks using a front kick to the stomach (3-4), followed by a straight punch to the face (5-6).

Demura faces his opponent in an uneven lead (1). Demura uses his right hand to close the distance (2) and bring the opponent's left hand down (3), creating an open angle to attack (4) with a backfist to the temple (5-6).

空手術

73

Demura squares off against his opponent (1). The opponent steps in (2) to launch an attack with the right hand (3) that Demura deflects with his left hand, as he simultaneously counterattacks with a chudan gyaku-tsuki (4).

Fumio Demura faces his opponent (1). The opponent attacks with a front kick (2) that Demura blocks with his left hand (3). This unbalances his opponent (4), and he applies a shuto-uchi to the neck (5-6).

空手術

Demura Sensei squares off against his opponent (1). As soon as the opponent initiates his attack, Demura Sensei moves his left leg back (2) to block the reverse punch using a shotei-uke (3). Then, he moves his body forward (4) and applies a palm attack to the opponent's chin (5).

Demura Sensei faces his opponent on uneven lead (1). When Demura feels his opponent advance, he brings his left leg back to create distance (2), and begins to move his left hand forward (3) to simultaneously deflect the attack and hit the opponent's eye with a finger jab (4).

空手術

77

Demura Sensei squares off against his opponent (1). When the opponent initiates his attack, Demura Sensei steps back to create distance (2), and turns around using otoshi-uke to block the incoming punch (3). Then, he locks the opponent's attacking arm (4), and applies an elbow attack to the opponent's back (5).

Demura Sensei faces his aggressor (1). As soon as the aggressor tries to move in, Demura steps back (2) and keep his body straight (3). Then, he lowers his stance for stability as he grabs the aggressor's hair (4) to control him (5) and applies a downward elbow attack (6) that brings the opponent to the ground (7).

79

Demura Sensei is facing his opponent (1). The aggressor grabs Demura's left leg (2). Demura Sensei pushes the opponent's body down as he applies forward pressure with his left knee (3) to unbalance the opponent (4). Then he prepares his posture (5) to finish the aggressor off with a punch to the face (6).

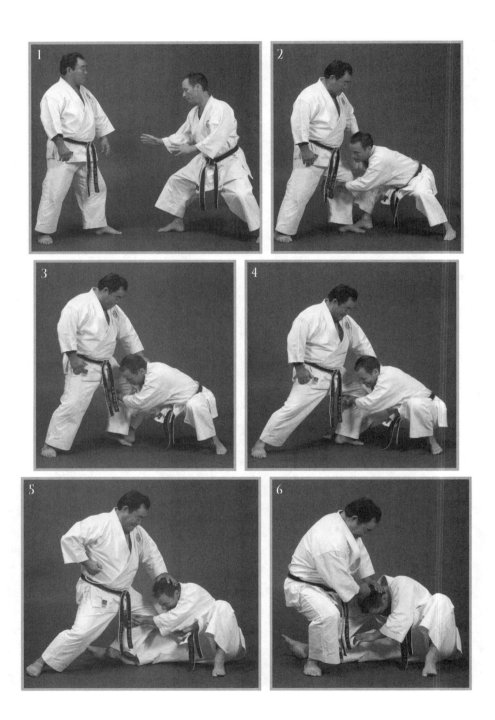

Demura squares off against his opponent (1). When the opponent attacks with an oi-tsuki (2), Demura steps back, uses his left hand to block the punch (3), and he follows with a reverse punch to the face (4) and a sokuto-geri to the knee of the opponent's right leg (5-6).

MORIO HIGAONNA

GOJU-RYU

He is a master, he is a warrior, he is one of the most charismatic karate instructors in the entire world. Born in 1940 as the son of a policeman, Sensei Higaonna's amazing knowledge of both karate and goju-ryu history has confounded practitioners from all styles and disciplines. His power, speed and quick smile are second to none. He is a living example to all karate practitioners of how the art can shape a man into a warrior. His goal, though, has never been to glorify himself. Instead, it's to preserve and perpetuate the traditional teachings he learned in Chojun Miyagi's famous garden dojo.

As his attacker punches, Higaonna Sensei blocks low and counters with
a strike to the throat (1). He follows this up with a backfist to the face (2), a face
claw strike (3) and another strike to the face (4-5). This is followed by a double
palm strike to both sides of the chin (6), which knocks his attacker down (7).
On the ground, he follows up with a kakato-geri to the groin (8) and an elbow
strike to the lower stomach (9).

Master Higaonna faces his opponent (1). As the opponent attacks with a front punch, Higaonna sidesteps and applies an outside block (2), followed by a shuto-uchi to the neck (3). Then he delivers a haito-uchi (5) that serves as the entry (6) for a takedown. He finished with a downward heel kick to the solar plexus (7).

85

Higaonna Sensei faces his opponent (1). When the opponent attacks with a forward punch, Higaonna Sensei blocks with both hands (2) and uses his left hand to bring the opponent's attacking arm down (3), which opens space for an uppercut to the chin (4). Then he grabs the opponent's neck, bringing his head down, and applies a knee strike to the face (5). Immediately, Master Higaonna squats and grabs the opponent's right leg (6), throwing him to the ground (7) so he can apply a final attack to the face (8).

1

Higaonna Sensei is grabbed from behind (1). He uses his left hand (2) to apply a groin strike from the back (3). Immediately, he applies pressure with his body to unbalance the opponent (4), as he uses his left hand to pull the aggressor's right elbow down (5). Then he brings his left leg to the front (6), and by lowering his body (7), throws the opponent onto the ground (8), where he controls him with an armbar as he simultaneously hits the face with the left knee (9).

2

3

4

5

6

7

8

9

87

Higaonna Sensei faces his opponent (1). As the opponent attacks, Higaonna steps back and blocks the attack with his left hand (2). Then he follows with an upward elbow strike to the face (3-4), a side elbow strike to the chin (5-6),

and a backward strike to the right side of the opponent's head (7). Immediately, he pushes the opponent (8-9) to the ground (10), where he finishes him off with a heel kick to the groin (11) and a double ippon-ken to the stomach (12).

空手術

The aggressor grabs Master Higaonna (1). Higaonna Sensei immediately attacks with a finger jab to the eyes (2), followed by a groin kick (3) and a downward elbow strike to break the grip (4). Then he grabs the opponent's right arm (5) and starts twisting it (6), until he gets an armbar that brings the opponent down (7). In a superior position, Higaonna Sensei applies (8) a final downward elbow strike to the back (9).

Higaonna Sensei squares off against his opponent (1). When the opponent tries to hit Master Higaonna with a hook, Sensei blocks with his left hand and simultaneously hits the opponent's stomach with an uppercut (2). Then, he uses another uppercut to hit the chin (3), a side circular elbow strike to the face (4) and a backward elbow strike to finish the opponent off (5).

91

Higaonna Sensei faces his opponent (1). As soon as the aggressor tries for a takedown, Higaonna Sensei steps back (2) and uses his arms to block the action (3). By placing his left arm under the opponent's right and using his left hand to grab the neck (4), Higaonna Sensei throws the opponent onto the ground (5), where he will finish him off with a final strike (6).

Master Higaonna squares off against his opponent (1). The opponent attacks with a front kick that Higaonna Sensei deflects with his left hand (2). He hooks the attacking leg and places his left hand on the opponent's throat (3). Then he lifts the right arm and grabs the opponent's gi (4) to lift him up (5). He lets him land on his left knee for a fatal strike (6).

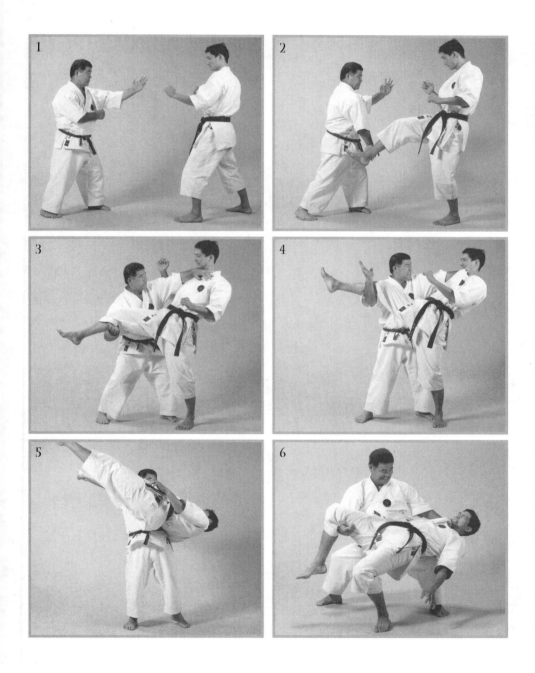

空手術

HIDEHARU IGAKI

SHITO-RYU

A traditional Japanese karate master who came to America to spread the art of the empty hand, Sensei Igaki has adapted the rigorous methods of traditional Eastern learning into a Western teaching system that challenges his students without driving them away. Driven by a true love of karate training and the Budo lifestyle, Sensei Igaki passes along his enthusiasm to all those he meets. He is spreading the Budo spirit to an entirely new generation of Western practitioners and proving in the process that the Budo spirit has universal appeal and application.

空手術

Igaki Sensei squares off against Stephen Heyl (1). Igaki closes the distance with a mae-tsuki (2). As Stephen moves backward to create more distance, Igaki Sensei attacks with gyaku-tsuki (3) and follows with a mae-jodan-mawashi-geri (4).

Igaki and Heyl face each other (1). Igaki Sensei attacks with a gyaku-tsuki chu-dan (2), followed with a feint of jodan mawashi-geri to open the angle (3), This allows him to get into close range (4), take his opponent down (5) and score with a final punch (6).

空手術

97

Igaki Sensei and Stephen Heyl face each other on guard (1). Igaki attacks with a jodan mawashi-geri (2) to close to the right distance (3). Then, he brings his opponent down (4) and finishes him with a punch (5).

Both fighters face each other on guard (1). Igaki Sensei suddenly closes the distance with a gyaku-tsuki (2) that covers his entry into close range (3). He then brings his opponent down (4) and scores with a punch (5).

99

Heyl and Igaki Sensei face each other on guard (1). Heyl attacks with a mae-tsuki, which Igaki parries (2). Igaki Sensei then avoids the kick by angling to the left (3) and then scores with a gyaku-tsuki chudan (4).

Igaki Sensei squares off against his opponent (1). The opponent closes the distance using a mae-tsuki (2). Igaki Sensei reacts to this by creating distance and blocking with his left hand (3). He immediately gains space, pulls his opponent's left hand (4), sweeps him from the outside (4), and brings him down to the ground (6), where he scores with a punch (7).

101

Heyl and Igaki Sensei face each other (1). Igaki attacks with a jodan mawashi-geri (2) that Heyl evades by moving his body back. At the same time, he keeps his feet in the same place to rapidly counterattack (3). Igaki senses the counter and converts his previous kick into a ura-mawashi-geri jodan that hits his opponent's head on the way in (4).

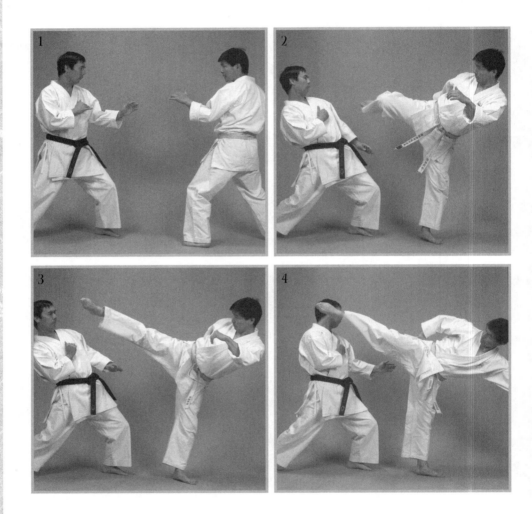

Igaki Sensei Squares against his opponent (1). The opponent attacks with a mae-tsuki that Igaki blocks with his right hand (2). When the opponent throws a reverse punch, Igaki uses his left hand to parry (3). He then enters into close range by stepping with his right leg (4). He sweeps his opponent to the ground and finishes him off with a punch to the stomach (5).

DAN IVAN

SHOTOKAN

A half-century of Budo experience is contained within this Old-World gentleman who is responsible for bringing some of the greatest Japanese karate masters of all time to the United States. His training under such notables as Isao Obata, Gogen Yamaguchi, Gozo Shioda, and Ryusho Sakagami—just to name a few—makes practitioners around the world, who would give up their firstborn for 10 percent of this man's experiences, look at him with healthy envy. Still fit and vital with a sharp, inquiring mind, Ivan enjoys sharing his experiences and knowledge with those lucky enough to come in contact with him.

Dan Ivan squares off against his opponent (1). When the opponent attacks with a forward punch, Ivan Sensei side steps and deflects the punch with his left hand (2). Then he uses the same hand to control the opponent's head (3), and push him back (4). Now, he applies a knee strike to the stomach (5), followed by an outside sweep (6).

Ivan Sensei faces his aggressor (1). As soon as the aggressor steps in to push Ivan Sensei (2), he lifts his arms and brings them down so he can block the incoming action (3). Immediately, he follows with a double-palm strike to the face (4), a knee to the stomach (5) and a downward elbow to the back (6).

Ivan Sensei feels the aggressor coming close from behind (1). When the aggressor grabs Ivan (2), Sensei turns around (3) and hooks both of the opponent's arms (4), securing them to apply a punch to the face (5), followed by a knee to the stomach (6).

Ivan Sensei squares off against his opponent (1). When the opponent attacks with a forward punch, Ivan Sensei side-steps to the left and deflects the punch (2). Then, he lifts his right knee (3) to deliver a roundhouse kick to the stomach (4). As he controls the attacking arm (5), Ivan Sensei delivers a strike to the opponent's elbow (6). He finally switches controls and applies a backfist to the face (7).

Ivan Sensei faces his opponent (1). When the opponent attacks with a forward punch, Ivan Sensei sidesteps and deflects the incoming blow (2), following with an elbow strike to the face (3). Immediately, he grabs the opponent's right wrist (4) and turns around to (5) apply a wristlock (6), which brings the aggressor to the ground for a final blow (7).

Ivan faces his opponent (1). As soon as the opponent attacks with a forward punch, Dan Ivan evades the attack and blocks the punch with his left hand (2). He immediately follows with an outside sweep (3-4), which brings the aggressor to the ground (6), where Sensei Ivan controls him (7).

Ivan Sensei squares off against his opponent (1). The opponent attacks with a straight punch to the face that is blocked by Ivan Sensei with his right hand (2). Immediately, he switches control using his left hand (3) and delivers an attack to the face (4) in the form of a shuto-uchi (5).

The attacker knocks Ivan Sensei down (1). Ivan uses his leg to stop any action (2), and while he hooks one leg behind the opponent's ankle, he kicks the other knee (3), bringing the opponent down (4), where he finishes (5) him with a kakato-geri to the groin (6).

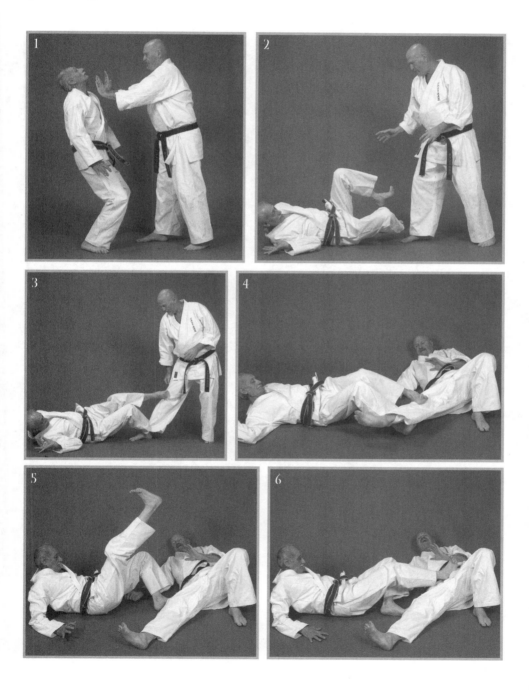

113

The aggressor controls Ivan Sensei from the mount position (1). Dan Ivan hits the opponent's ribcage to release the grip (2) and then pulls both arms up to bring the opponent's body close to him (3). Once the opponent is out of balance, he turns to the side (4) and breaks free from the control, preparing his counter (5), which is an elbow strike to the face as he ends up on top (6).

Ivan Sensei is pushed from behind (1) and ends up on the ground (2). As soon as he lands, Ivan Sensei turns around and kicks his opponent in the groin using an ushiro-geri (3). Then he hooks the opponent's right leg using both feet (4) and brings him down (5) to the ground (6), where he takes the advantage and prepares to deliver (7) a final kakato-geri to the stomach (8).

Ivan Sensei is seated in seiza (1) when the aggressor initiates his attack. Ivan Sensei reacts by grabbing both feet and hitting the opponent's groin with his head (2). Then he pulls, with his left hand, the opponent's right ankle (3), which brings the aggressor to the ground (4), where Ivan Sensei adopts a superior position (5) and delivers a final punch to the groin (6).

Sensei Ivan squares off against his opponent (1). The opponent attacks by using an outside sweep (2), which brings Ivan Sensei to the ground (3). As soon as the opponent leans forward to punch, Ivan Sensei attacks with a mawashi-geri from the ground (4). He then hooks the opponent's right leg with both feet (5), bringing him down to the ground (6), where he finishes the counterattack with a kick to the face (7-8).

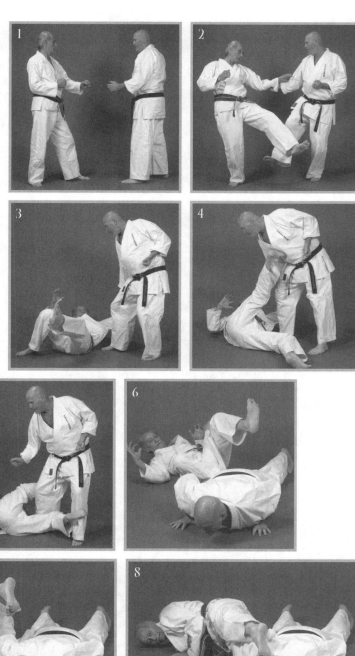

HIROKAZU KANAZAWA

SHOTOKAN

Sensei Kanazawa was the second person to graduate from the JKA Instructor Training Program, and many consider him to be one of the most skillful fighters of all time. Tempered by years of strict and difficult practice, his body reflects the decades of grueling karate training and conditioning. It is said that training with a true master is the only way to fully understand karate-do. Hirokazu Kanazawa is one of those rare teachers who possess the ability to pass both the spiritual and physical essence of the art.

Kanazawa Sensei squares off against his opponent (1). When the opponent initiates his attack (2), Kanazawa uses tai-sabaki to neutralize the punch and simultaneously counters with mae-tsuki (3). Then he retracts his front foot to gain distance and momentum (4) for a gyaku-tsuki chudan (5). As soon as the fist impacts with the target, Kanazawa Sensei uses his left hand to push the opponent' arms away. This prevents any other attack (6-7).

Facing his opponent (1), Kanazawa Sensei deflects the attacking yoko-geri (2) to his left side (3), creating an opening (4), which allows him to finish his opponent with a powerful ushiro-geri to the face (5).

121

Kanazawa Sensei faces the aggressor (1). As his opponent assumes a position to attack with a front kick (2), Kanazawa Sensei adjusts the distance and blocks the kick (3). He then sets himself (4) and finishes with a final double-hand counterattack to the opponent's neck (5).

Kanazawa Sensei faces his opponent (1). The opponent assumes an attacking position (2) and throws a forward punch to the face that is blocked by Hirokazu Kanazawa with a shuto-uke (3). He follows that with a jodan shuto-uchi to the side of the neck (4).

123

Kanazawa Sensei squares off against his opponent (1). As soon as the opponent initiates his front kick, Kanazawa Sensei steps in with a double-hand block (2). Then he slides his left hand forward and hits the opponent's neck as sidesteps to the left (3-4). Immediately, Kanazawa Sensei steps back to assume zanchin (5).

Kanazawa Sensei squares off against his opponent (1). The opponent attacks with a jodan mawashi-geri (2), which is deflected by a double-knife hand block (3), followed by a right roundhouse kick to the face (4). Then Kanazawa Sensei steps back to zanchin (5).

125

TAK KUBOTA

GOSOKU-RYU

Takayuki Kubota is one of the most famous and respected karate masters in the United States. In addition to teaching his very aggressive style of gosoku-ryu karate, Sensei Kubota has been acknowledged as the most active and innovative karate instructor in the field of law enforcement techniques. Although his hair has grayed some since his memorable Long Beach demonstration in the mid-1960s, he still leads his classes with the same intensity and dedication he did then. Someone said once that if you threw all the top masters in the world into one room and had them fight, Kubota would be the one who walked out.

Kubota Sensei squares off against his opponent (1). When the opponent attacks with a forward punch, Kubota deflects the attack using a parry with his left hand (2) and a check with his right (3), and immediately counters with a reverse punch to the ribcage (4).

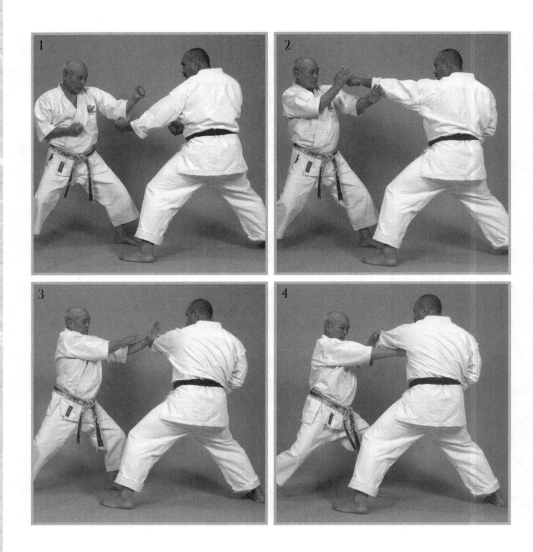

Kubota faces his opponent (1). The opponent attacks with a roundhouse kick that Kubota Sensei blocks (2). Then he grabs the attacking leg with his left arm (3) and delivers a final gyaku-tsuki to the stomach (4).

Kubota Sensei squares off against his opponent (1). As soon as the opponent initiates his attack with a front kick, Kubota Sensei steps in and deflects the kick with his left hand as he simultaneously punches to the stomach with his right (2). Then he grabs the kicking leg (3) and brings his right leg inside (4) to sweep the opponent (5), taking him to the ground, where he finishes him off with a punch (6).

Kubota Sensei faces the aggressor (1). The aggressor attacks with a kick that is blocked by Kubota Sensei (2). He follows with a punch to the face (3), a kick to the groin (4) and a final backfist to the temple (5-6).

131

Kubota Sensei squares off against his aggressor (1). As the opponent steps in to attack, Kubota Sensei sidesteps (2) and blocks the attack with the right hand. Simultaneously, he uses his left arm to hit the aggressor's right elbow (3), which releases the grip. He then applies a disarm (4), followed by a hit to the stomach (5), and a second counterattack to the ribcage (6).

The attacker faces Kubota Sensei (1). As soon as the attacker initiates his movement (2), Kubota Sensei circles to the right and evades the strike (3), grabbing the aggressor by the neck and right arm (4), which takes him down to the ground (5-6), where he applies a final kick to the face (7).

Kubota Sensei, with an umbrella in his hand, faces the aggressor (1). As soon as the aggressor grabs Kubota's lapel (2), Sensei swings the umbrella (3), and hits the aggressor in the face (4), followed by a hit to the stomach (5) and a new strike to the back of the neck (6).

Kubota Sensei faces his opponent (1). The opponent begins to attack with a knife to which Kubota Sensei reacts by opening his arms to facilitate (2) the movement to the side and the blocking action (3). Immediately, Kubota Sensei takes control of the attacking arm (4), and applies a shuto-uchi to the opponent's neck (5).

PATRICK McCARTHY

KORYU UCHINADI

Patrick McCarthy has spent much of his life practicing, studying, researching and writing about karate. A world traveler who has personally sought the secret kata of karate's remaining "old" masters, McCarthy is also a gifted academia who spent nine years translating "The Bible of Karate," the Bubishi, the most important historical karate discovery of our time, into English. McCarthy's diligent research serves as a reminder that karate, or any martial art for that matter, can never be mastered without the guidance of some-one who knows the way.

The aggressor grabs McCarthy Sensei by the neck (1). He uses his left hand to release the grip (2), strikes with a finger jab to the throat (3) and moves his right hand to open the angle. He pushes the opponent's left arm to the side (4-5) to apply a bent armlock (6). Reverse angle (7).

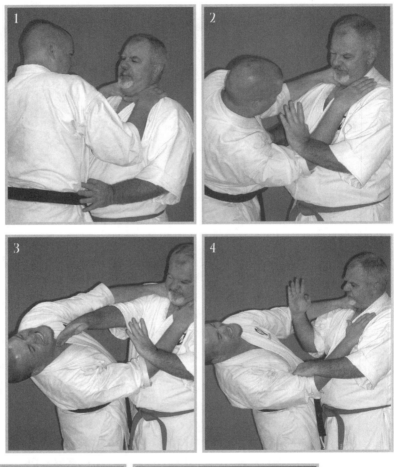

The aggressor gets close to McCarthy Sensei (1), steps in and grabs him (2). Immediately, McCarthy Sensei uses his right elbow to hit the opponent's neck (3), which releases the grip and allows him to apply an armbar as (4). He simultaneously delivers a low sidekick to the back of the opponent's right leg (5).

The aggressor grabs McCarthy Sensei's lapel (1). Using his left forearm, Sensei strikes the opponent's left arm (2). As soon as the aggressor attacks again with a right punch, McCarthy Sensei blocks with his left hand (3). Then he reverse the control of the opponent's attacking arm to the right hand and applies an armbar (4), followed by a kick to the inside of the opponent's left leg (5) and an uppercut to the chin (6).

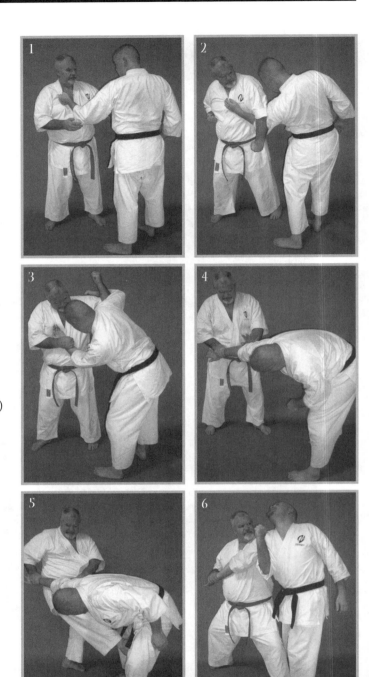

The aggressor starts his attack (1). McCarthy Sensei uses his right hand to deflect the incoming attack (2) and grabs the aggressor right wrist (3). Then he applies a palm strike to the face (4) and finishes with an elbow wrench (5).

The aggressor grabs McCarthy Sensei by both lapels (1). Sensei grabs the attacker's head and delivers an uppercut to the chin (2), followed by a twist of the neck and a tettsui-uchi strike to the face (3). Close-up (4).

The aggressor grabs McCarthy Sensei from behind (1). Sensei applies a foot stomp to release the grip (2), opens his stance to a siko-dachi (3) and brings his arm to the back (4) to apply a headbutt to the opponent's face (5), followed by a downward arm movement that liberates him from the attack (6).

The aggressor grabs McCarthy Sensei by the shoulders (1). Sensei turns around (2) and passes his head under the opponent's arms (3), which forces the opponent to cross his arms (4). Then he applies a powerful strike to the face as he simultaneously controls the opponent's right arm (5).

The aggressor grabs McCarthy Sensei's lapel (1). Sensei immediately kicks the opponent in the groin with a front kick (2), and follows with an elbow wrench (3) and a downward elbow attack to the opponent's neck (4).

145

The aggressor grabs McCarthy Sensei from behind (1). Sensei uses a headbutt to release the pressure (2). Then he turns around (3) and applies a painful armbar on opponent's right arm (4).

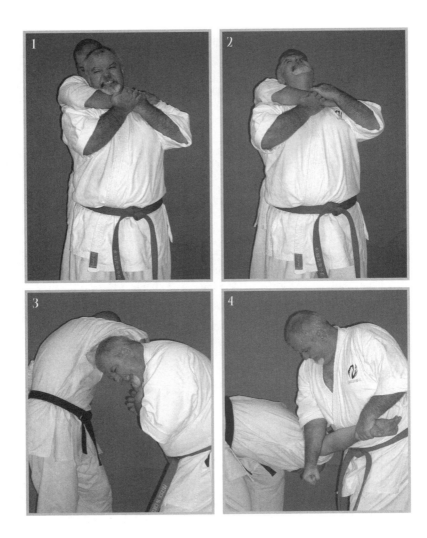

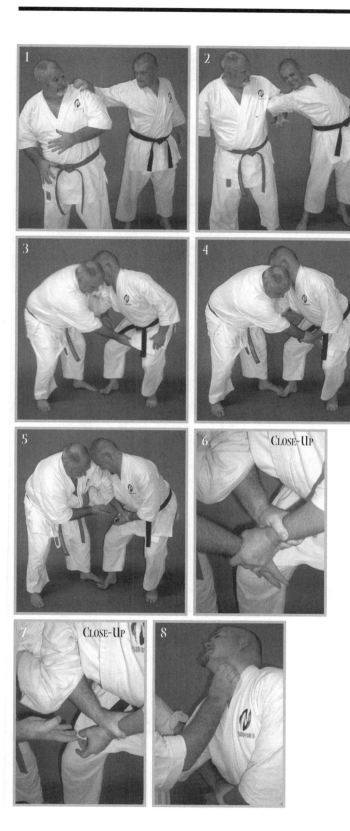

The aggressor grabs McCarthy Sensei by the left shoulder (1). Sensei turns around and hooks the attacking arm with his own left arm (2), then he steps in and applies a palm strike to the groin (3), which is blocked by the opponent (4). McCarthy Sensei uses his left hand to break free from the opponent's grip (5), as shown in close-ups (6-7). Then he finishes the opponent off with an attack to the throat (8).

The aggressor grabs McCarthy Sensei (1). Sensei steps back with his right leg and delivers a palm strike to the groin (2). Then he grabs the opponent's left hand (3) and applies a wristlock (4). Reverse angle (5).

REVERSE ANGLE

The aggressor grabs McCarthy Sensei from behind, trying to apply a choke (1). Sensei uses his right hand to release the grip (2), and then he switches to his left hand (3). Then he turns around to reverse the choke into a wristlock-armbar combination (4).

The aggressor grabs McCarthy Sensei by the head and delivers an upward knee strike, which is blocked by Sensei suing both hands (1). McCarthy Sensei uses his left hand to grab the opponent's leg (3), gets close to him (4), and applies a sweep to the supporting leg (4), which brings the opponent to the ground where he finishes with a punch (5).

The aggressor grabs McCarthy Sensei from behind (1). Sensei delivers a strike to the opponent's groin (2), turns around to the right (3), and grabs the opponent's right hand (4). Then he switches grips (5), and breaks his right hand free (6) to deliver a punch to the face (7).

CHUCK MERRIMAN

GOJU-RYU

Chuck Merriman's karate career began in 1960 and within a few years he had become one of the leading figures in American karate and the personal bodyguard for stars such as Diana Ross and the rock group Kiss. He managed the first professional, corporate-sponsored karate team, which competed across the globe in the 1980s. His evolution as martial artist led him to train with Okinawa's Sensei Miyazato Eiichi in the traditional goju-ryu style. Sensei Merriman's goal is not only to produce good karateka, but also to produce better human beings in the process.

Merriman Sensei faces an armed opponent (1). The aggressor attacks with a knife to the stomach. Merriman Sensei reacts by sidestepping and deflecting the arm with his left forearm (2). Then he grabs the attacking arm with his right hand and applies a final elbow strike to the ribcage (3).

Merriman Sensei squares off against his opponent (1). The opponent attacks with a hook to the face that Merriman blocks with his left hand (2). Then he counterattacks with an uppercut to the chin (3) and controls the opponent by grabbing his throat (4).

空手術

155

Merriman Sensei faces his armed attacker (1). The aggressor steps in and attacks with a club. Merriman Sensei blocks the attack with both hands (2), grabs the opponent's wrist and turns around (3) to apply an elbow wrench (4).

Chuck Merriman faces his opponent (1). When the opponent launches a front kick attack, Merriman Sensei sidesteps and hooks the opponent's leg with his right arm as he simultaneously applies an elbow strike to the ribcage (2). Then he sweeps the opponent, bringing him to the ground, and applies the final attack (3).

Merriman Sensei squares off against his opponent (1). The opponent attacks with a forward punch that Merriman Sensei deflects by sidestepping to the left and applying a shuto-uke (2). Then he grabs the opponent's right wrist and applies a sokuto-geri to the back of the opponent's right knee (3).

Facing his opponent (1) Merriman Sensei blocks the gyaku-tsuki chudan with his left hand (2) and the left hook with his right hand (3). He then uses his left hand (4) to position himself on the outside of his opponent (5), where he grabs the wrist of the extended arm (6) and strikes the aggressor's elbow joint (7).

Merriman Sensei faces the aggressor (1). When the opponent attacks with a left punch, Merriman Sensei blocks with his right hand (2). As soon as the aggressor attacks with a hook to the body, Sensei blocks with his left hand and hits the biceps with an elbow strike (3), as he simultaneously puts pressure on the opponent's left knee with his right leg (4).

Merriman Sensei faces his opponent (1). When the opponent attacks with a left punch, Sensei Merriman blocks with both hands (2). Then he blocks the right-hand punch with a soto-uke (3), controls the opponent's attacking arm with his left (4) and applies a final backfist to the temple (5).

161

Merriman Sensei faces his opponent (1). Grabbed by the wrist (2), he traps the wrist (3) and pressures the joint upwards (4). When the aggressor attacks with a reverse punch, Merriman Sensei blocks with the palm of his left hand (5) and delivers an ura-ken to the temple (6-7).

Merriman Sensei faces his opponent (1). The aggressor grabs Sensei's left wrist (2). Merriman answers by stepping to the side and using his right elbow to dissolve the grip (3), as he simultaneously applies a sokuto-geri to the back of the knee (4).

Merriman Sensei faces his aggressor (1). The aggressor attacks with a straight punch that is blocked by Merriman Sensei's left hand (2). Then he strikes the opponent's elbow (3), followed by a check of the attacking arm with his left hand (4) and a final ura-ken to the face (5).

The aggressor grabs Sensei Merriman's right wrist (1). Sensei holds the opponent's grabbing hand and moves his body to the side (2), which creates leverage to apply a painful wristlock (3). Then he brings his body down into a siko-dachi stance (4), so he can apply a ura-ken to the back of the opponent's head (5-6).

Merriman Sensei faces his opponent (1). He blocks the opponent's left-hand punch (2). When the aggressor attacks with a new punch, Merriman sidesteps to the left, blocks the punch (3) and applies a side kick to the back of the leg (4).

Chuck Merriman faces his opponent (1). The aggressor grabs Merriman's wrists (2). Sensei steps back and brings both hands up (3), then he open the arms and strikes with his head to the opponent's face (3). Once the opponent has lost his balance (5), he brings his hands up and uses his right hand to break the grip (6), as shown in detail (7), to apply a final strike to the armpit (8).

DETAIL

167

An opponent faces Merriman Sensei (1) and takes a stance to attack (2). Merriman Sensei blocks the forward punch with his right hand (3) and counterattacks with ura-tsuki to the stomach (4), followed by an outside sweep (5) and a kick to the face (6).

An opponent faces Merriman Sensei (1) and takes a stance to attack (2). Merriman Sensei blocks the forward punch with his right hand (3) and follows with a reverse punch to the stomach (4). Then he steps to the left side (5) and applies a sidekick to the inside of the opponent's left knee (6).

169

Merriman Sensei faces the opponent (1). The aggressor attacks with a forward punch that is blocked by Merriman Sensei with his forearm (2). Then he counterattacks with a backfist to the face (3). Merriman Sensei grabs the opponent's neck (3), applies an uppercut to the body (4) and grabs the aggressor's right arm (5) to apply an armbar (6). Detail (7).

Merriman Sensei squares off against the opponent (1). When the opponent attacks with a forward punch, Merriman Sensei blocks with his left hand (2) and delivers a haito-uchi to the ribcage (3). The opponent still launches a new attack that is blocked by Merriman Sensei with his right hand (4). Detail (5). Then he moves the attacking arm to the other side and delivers a punch to the face (6).

VAL MIJAILOVIC

GOSOKU-RYU

Val Mijailovic is the kind of fighter that you'd be glad was on your side if you got jumped in a dark alley. A direct student of Tak Kubota, Sensei Mijailovic is as powerful with his words as he is with his fists. With a natural talent for the finer points of the art, he stresses that attitude is the major factor to be successful in the way of true karate-do. As a competitor, he has gathered many of the most important trophies in the karate circles, including the first IKA World Cup title. After many years of dedication he still shows his loyalty to his sensei and the ethical code of the warrior, Sensei Mijailovic devotes much of his current time to the martial arts.

Mijailovic Sensei squares off against his opponent (1). He steps in with an outside sweep feint (2), followed by a inside sweep with his right foot (3), which unbalances his opponent (4) and brings him down (5), where Mijailovic applies a final downward elbow to the back (6-7).

Mijailovic Sensei closes the distance using mae-tsuki (1), followed by a reverse punch to the face (2), which he uses to get close to the opponent (3). This enables him to throw the opponent (4-5) onto the ground, where he finishes him off (6) with a punch to the face (7).

175

Mijailovic Sensei faces his opponent (1). When the opponent attacks, Mijailovic Sensei closes the distance and punches with his left hand inside the opponent's punch (2). Then he grabs the opponent's left arm and sweeps him from the outside (3), moves to the back (4) and applies a rear choke (5) to finish his opponent (6).

Mijailovic Sensei squares off against his opponent. When the opponent attacks with mae-tsuki (1), Mijailovic Sensei steps to the left side and blocks the punch with his left hand (2), following with an outside sweep (3), which brings the opponent onto the ground (4), where he finishes off with a punch to the face (5).

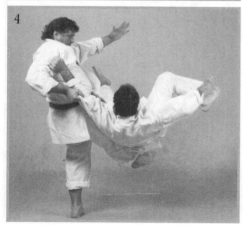

Mijailovic Sensei squares off against his opponent (1). Sensei moves his right foot close to his left to gain momentum (2), as he closes the distance and covers the entry with his hands (3). Then he uses his left leg to apply a powerful sweep (4), which lifts the opponent into the air (5). He lands on the ground and Sensei throws the finishing punch (6).

Mijailovic Sensei squares off against his opponent (1). He closes the distance with mae-tsuki (2), a reverse punch that hits the target (3-4), and an inside sweep (5) that brings the opponent onto the ground (6). He finishes him off with a side-kick to the face (7-8).

Val Mijailovic faces his opponent (1). He closes the distance and uses his right hand to cover the entry (2), as he punches with mae-tsuki (3) and finishes with gyaku-tsuki to the face (4).

Mijailovic Sensei squares off against his opponent (1). Sensei closes the distance and slaps the opponent's lead hand to create an opening (2) for the final kick to the face (3).

181

Mijailovic Sensei faces the opponent (1). When the opponent starts the front kick attack, Mijailovic Sensei uses his left leg to block the kick to the outside (2). Then he keeps "pushing" the leg away from the opponent's body (3) and scores with a punch to the face (4).

Val Mijailovic faces his aggressor (1). When the aggressor initiates his attack using a reverse punch to the stomach, Mijailovic Sensei steps in, parries with his left hand (2), and before the opponent delivers a round-house kick, Sensei strikes with a shuto-uchi to the side of the neck (3).

183

Mijailovic Sensei squares off against his opponent (1). Sensei moves his left foot to the side (2) to create balance and leverage to apply an inside sweep (3). Once the attacker is off balance, Sensei strikes with gyaku-tsuki to the face (4).

Mijailovic Sensei faces his opponent (1). The opponent steps in and attacks with a reverse punch that Mijailovic Sensei deflects with his left hand (2). He then counterattacks with a right shuto-uchi to the temple (3).

Mijailovic Sensei faces his opponent (1). When the opponent starts the attack with a front kick, Mijailovic Sensei sidesteps to the left and blocks with his right hand (2). Then he brings his right leg behind the opponent's left leg (3) to sweep and take him to the ground (4).

Val Mijailovic faces his opponent (1). He steps in and closes the distance while covering the entry with his left hand (2). He finally hits the target with a clean gyaku-tsuki to the face (3).

Mijailovic Sensei squares off against his opponent (1). He closes the distance and uses his right hand to slap the opponent's left hand (2). This creates an opening for a powerful front kick to the stomach (3), followed by a reverse punch to the face (4).

Mijailovic Sensei faces his opponent (1). He closes the distance and attacks with a reverse punch to the face (2), followed by a sweep using his right leg (3), which brings his opponent to the ground for a final punch (4).

Mijailovic Sensei squares off against his opponent (1). He steps in and closes the distance, covering the entry with his right hand (2). Then he uses an inside sweep to open the angle (3) for a final punch to the face (4).

Mijailovic Sensei squares off against his opponent (1). He steps in and closes the distance, covering the entry with his left hand (2). Then he uses his left leg to apply an inside sweep to open the angle (3) for a final punch to the face (4).

191

Val Mijailovic squares against his opponent (1). He opens his guard to draw the opponent's attack (2). The opponent's moves in with a reverse punch (2), which is blocked by Mijailovic Sensei's right hand and countered with a mae-tsuki to the face (4).

Mijailovic Sensei squares off against his opponent (1). He steps in and closes the distance, covering the entry with both hands (2). Then he uses his right leg to apply an inside sweep as he simultaneously applies a punch to the face (3) and follows with another right-hand punch (4).

空手術

MINOBU MIKI

SHITO-RYU

One of the world's highest-ranking shito-ryu stylists, Minobu Miki is from a Japanese family steeped in the traditional aspects of the martial arts. Known for his very technical and precise knowledge of every aspect of the art, Miki Sensei recognizes the need to modernize karate's traditionally harsh training methods while remaining true to the art's high spiritual and moral principles. With one foot planted in the past and the other rooted in the present, Minobu Miki is a living example of how karate's honorable traditions can survive the modern world's questionable values.

Miki Sensei squares off against his opponent (1). He steps forward with an oi-tsuki to the face (2), followed by a gyaku-tsuki chudan (3). Then he steps back to adjust the distance (4) and attacks with a final mawashi-geri to the face (5).

Miki Sensei faces his opponent (1). He steps in with a gyaku-tsuki chudan (2) and immediately moves back (3) to punch with his left hand (4). Then he brings the left knee up (5) and scores with a high roundhouse kick to the face (6).

空手術

197

Miki Sensei faces his opponent (1). The opponent attacks with a front kick that Minobu Miki deflects with his left hand, using sukui-uke (2), followed by a hand attack (3), using haito-uchi (4).

Miki Sensei squares off against his opponent (1). When the opponent attacks with an oi-tsuki, Miki Sensei blocks with his left hand (2) and follows with a palm strike to the chin (3) and shotei-uchi to the groin (4). Then he drops (5), turns around and throws the opponent to the ground (6), where he finishes him off with a punch to the face (7).

199

The opponent grabs Miki Sensei by the lapel (1). Sensei checks the grip with his left hand as he simultaneously attacks the opponent's eyes with a finger jab (2). Then he uses his right elbow to apply an armbar, which brings the opponent down (3); he passes his right leg over the aggressor's left arm (4), so he can push him all the way to the ground (5), where he controls the situation (6) and applies a final punch to the back of the head (7).

Miki Sensei squares off against his opponent (1). When the opponent steps in to grab both of Miki's lapels, Sensei Miki uses both arms (2) to stop the attack (3). Then he applies an upward knee strike to the chest (4) and a side-kick to the back of the opponent's right leg (5). He pulls him back (6), so he can take him to the ground, where he delivers the final punch to the stomach (7).

Miki Sensei is grabbed from behind (1). Sensei steps out with his left leg as he simultaneously hits the opponent's chest with a backward elbow (2), followed by an ura-ken to the face (3), a tettsui-uchi to the groin (4) and a throw (5), which brings the opponent to the ground, where Miki Sensei applies a final punch (6).

Miki Sensei squares off against the opponent (1). The aggressor tries to grab Miki by the waist to take him down. Miki Sensei reacts by stepping back with his left leg (2) and applying an upward elbow strike (3-4). Then he grabs the opponent's right thigh (5) and rolls back (6), bringing the aggressor to the ground (7), where he applies a kick to the face (8).

The opponent gets close to Miki Sensei (1) and grabs him from behind (2). Minobu Miki steps back with his left leg (3) and brings his left hand over the aggressor's face (4). Then he grabs the opponent's right leg and lifts him up (5), dropping him onto the floor (6), where he applies a decisive kick to the face (7-8).

Miki Sensei squares off against his opponent (1). The opponent attacks with a front kick that Miki Sensei deflects with a sukui-uke (2). Miki Sensei counters with a kin-geri to the groin (3). Then he grabs the opponent's right foot (4) and twists it to throw the aggressor to the ground (5), where he applies a final kick to the groin (6).

Miki Sensei faces his aggressor (1). The aggressor steps in to grab Miki Sensei's left leg. Sensei reacts by stepping back with his right leg (2) and striking with a downward elbow to the back of the head (3). Then he grabs the opponent's chin (4), twists it to throw him (5) to the ground and applies the final blow with a shuto-uchi to the throat (6-7).

Miki Sensei faces his opponent (1). The opponent grabs Miki Sensei's right wrist (2). Miki Sensei grabs the opponent's hand and turns it around (3) to create a wristlock (4). Then he follows with a front kick to the face (5) and an armbar on the ground (6).

207

Miki Sensei faces his opponent (1). When the opponent grabs both of Sensei Miki's wrists (2), he reacts by kicking with a kin-geri to the groin (3). Then he grabs both of the opponent wrists (4), turns around (5) and applies a throw (6-7), which ends with the aggressor on the ground (8), where Miki Sensei delivers the final blow (9).

Miki Sensei faces his opponent, who is armed with a club (1). When the opponent attacks, Miki Sensei blocks with both hands (2) and then brings his weight back (3) to counter with a jodan mawashi-geri (4), followed by a side kick to the opponent's right leg (5). Then he grabs the opponent's right arm (6), twists in a counterclockwise motion (7) and applies a throw (8), bringing the aggressor to the ground, where he takes the club out of his hand (9) and applies a final blow (10).

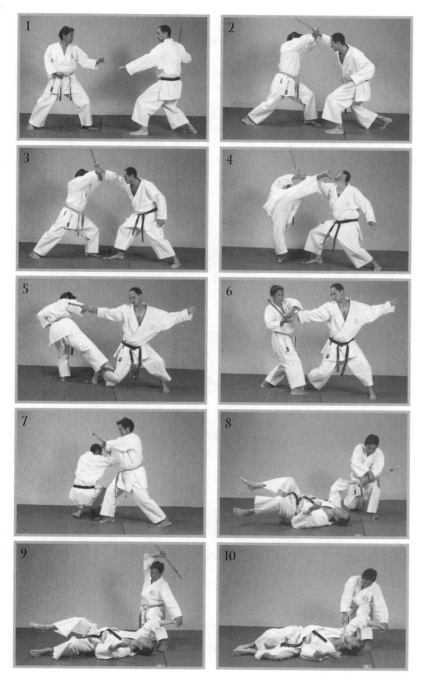

Miki Sensei is grabbed from behind (1). He opens his arms to the side to create space (2), and then he raises them (3-4) all the way (5). He suddenly drops and hits the opponent's face with the back of his head (6). He opens his stance even wider to throw off the aggressor's balance (7), and he steps forward as he simultaneously hits him in the groin (8). He then grabs his right wrist (9) and throws his opponent onto the ground (10-11), where he controls him with a wristlock (12).

210

空手術

KUNIO MIYAKE

SHITO-RYU

Miyake Sensei began teaching the martial arts in Japan while he was teaching modern Japanese language and literature at the high school level. He moved to the United States in 1985 and quickly established Shuko-Kai U.S.A. in Southern California with permission from Shuko-kai Tani-ha Shito-Ryu Soke Chojiro Tani. He was the All-Japanese champion in shito-ryu shuko-kai in 1982 and the 1988 U.S.A. Karate Federation National champion. Miyake Sensei has earned a high level of respect by sharing karate-do with love, empathy and dedication. He strives for a life of tranquility and contentment, refreshed by the satisfaction derived from pursuing the way of martial arts with discipline and commitment.

Miyake Sensei squares off against his opponent (1). The opponent initiates the attack with a mae-tsuki that is blocked by Miyake's left hand (2). Immediately, Miyake Sensei delivers a reverse punch to the stomach (3) and sweeps the opponent (4) onto the ground (5), where he delivers the final punch to the face (6).

Miyake Sensei faces his opponent (1). When the opponent attacks with a forward punch, Miyake blocks with his left hand (2), grabs the opponent's head and applies an uppercut to the face (3). Then he throws the opponent (4) onto the ground (5-6), where he finally delivers (7) the decisive punch to the ribcage (8).

215

Miyake Sensei squares off against his opponent (1). The opponent throws a roundhouse kick that Miyake intercepts by stepping in (2). Then he grabs the opponent's attacking leg (3) and uses his left leg (4) to throw the opponent to the ground (5), where he delivers a punch to the stomach (6).

Kunio Miyake faces his opponent (1). The opponent attacks with a reverse punch that is blocked by Miyake's gedan-barai (2). He follows with a gyaku-tsuki chudan (3). Then he brings his right hand around the opponent's neck (4) and throws him (5) to the ground (6), where he delivers the final punch to the stomach (7).

217

Miyake Sensei squares off against his opponent (1). The opponent attacks with a front kick that is blocked by Kunio Miyake (2). Then he grabs the attacking leg and moves his right leg inside (3) to throw the opponent to the ground, where he will deliver the final and decisive blow (4).

Miyake Sensei faces his opponent (1). The opponent attacks with mae-tsuki and Miyake sidesteps to the left (2) to counter with ura-mawashi-geri jodan (3). He follows with an outside sweep to the opponent's right leg (4-5) and a final punch to the stomach (6).

Miyake Sensei faces his opponent (1). The opponent attacks with a mae-tsuki that Miyake Sensei blocks with his right hand (2). Then he uses the left hand to block the opponent's gyaku-tsuki (3) and delivers the counterattack with an ura-ken to the temple (4).

Miyake Sensei squares off against his opponent (1). The opponent attacks with a front kick that is deflected by Miyake's sukui-uke (2). This not only pushes the attacking leg away, it unbalances the opponent's position (3) and weakens the punch with the right hand (4). Miyake Sensei controls the opponent's attacking arm and delivers a mae-tsuki to the face (5).

221

Miyake Sensei faces his opponent (1). The opponent attacks with a jodan mawashi-geri that Miyake Sensei blocks with a X-block (2). He then grabs the attacking leg (3) to bring the opponent to the ground (4-5), where he controls the opponent (6) and delivers the final punch to the opponent's back (7).

Miyake Sensei squares off against his opponent (1). Miyake Sensei closes the distance by using a feint of mae-tsuki (2). He then brings his right leg forward to sweep the opponent's left leg (2) and then moves to the right (4) to deliver a jodan mawashi-geri (5-6).

Miyake Sensei faces his opponent
(1). Miyake closes the distance and
uses his left hand to check the opponent's left hand (2). Then he delivers
a reverse punch to the face (3), followed
by a throw (4), which brings the opponent to the ground, where he can apply
the final punch to the stomach (5).

Miyake Sensei faces his opponent (1). The opponent attacks with a forward punch that Miyake blocks using a juji-uke (2). Then he grabs the opponent's attacking arm with his right hand (3) and converts the action into an armbar (4) to bring the opponent to the ground (5-6), where he applies a final backfist to the temple (7-8).

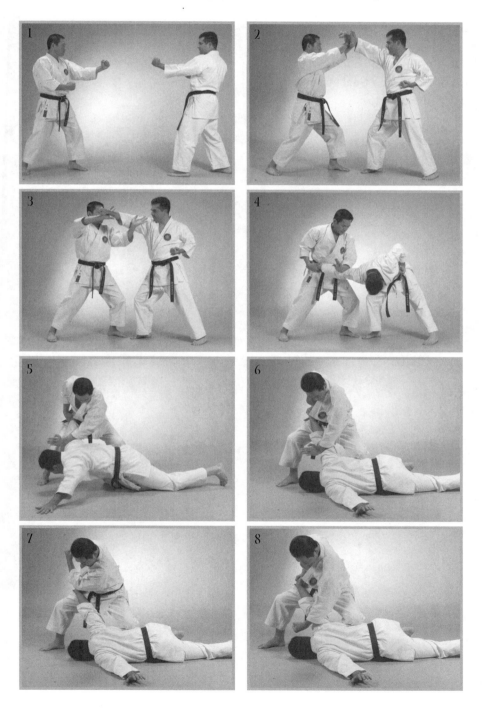

225

Kunio Miyake faces his opponent (1). The opponent attacks with a jodan mawashi-geri that Miyake Sensei parries with a X-block (2). He uses the block to control the attacking leg (3) and pushes it away so the opponent's body turns (4), which leaves a clear opening for a final gyaku-tsuki to the back (5).

Miyake Sensei squares off against his opponent (1). Using his left hand, Miyake blocks the attacker's forward punch (2). Then he follows with a palm strike to the chin (3) and moves his right leg to the outside for a sweep (4-5). With the opponent on the ground (6), Miyake Sensei delivers the final punch to the ribcage (7).

227

TOM MUZILA

SHOTOKAN

Sensei Muzila stands in the world today as one of a handful of privileged students of the great karate master Tsutomu Ohshima. From his early days, Muzila has been a man of conviction and discipline. Known among his peers for being an innovator and a well-respected writer, Tom Muzila had the opportunity of testing his bushido spirit as a former Green Beret, skydiver, fire-walker and mountain climber—besides all the high-intensity marathon training sessions that exemplify the mental discipline and self-effacement necessary in the samurai culture of feudal Japan.

Muzila Sensei squares off against his opponent (1). When the opponent initiates his attack, Muzila steps in (2) and positions himself to the outside of the attack (3), from where he can apply an outside sweep (4) to bring the opponent down to the ground for a final punch to the face (5).

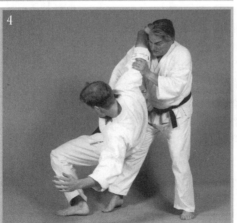

Muzila Sensei faces his opponent (1). The opponent attacks with a forward punch (2), which Muzila deflects by moving to the side (3). Then he moves behind the opponent (4) and applies a final armlock, which brings the opponent to the ground (5).

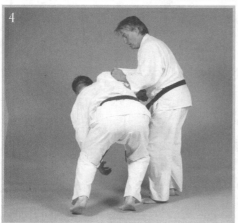

231

Tom Muzila squares off against his opponent (1). The opponent initiates the attack, and Muzila Sensei reacts by stepping in and passing his right arm over the opponent's left shoulder (2). He then applies a final choke from the side (3).

Muzila Sensei faces his opponent (1). When the opponent attacks, Muzila Sensei sidesteps and positions himself behind the attacker (2), from where he controls his body (3) and applies a choke-armlock combination (4).

233

Muzila Sensei squares off against his opponent (1). As soon as the opponent initiates the attack, Muzila Sensei steps in and intercepts the action by simultaneously blocking the attacking arm with his right hand and by grabbing the head with his left (2). Then he turns around and throws the opponent (3) onto the ground, where he applies a final punch (4).

Muzila Sensei faces his opponent (1). The opponent attacks with a forward punch to the face, which is blocked by Muzila's defense (2). Then he turns around (3) and applies a throw (4), which brings the aggressor onto the ground, where Muzila delivers the final punch (5).

235

Muzila Sensei faces his opponent (2). Sensei blocks the opponent's forward punch with his left hand (2). Then he brings his right arm under the opponent's right arm and simultaneously steps in (3) to position himself on the opponent's right side (4), where he applies a painful armbar (5).

Muzila Sensei squares off against his opponent (1). As soon as he feels the opponent is trying to grab him (2), Muzila Sensei moves under the opponent's arm, grabs him by the legs (3) and throws him on the ground (4). Here he applies a final punch to the stomach (5).

237

Muzila Sensei faces his opponent (1). When the opponent initiates his attack, Muzila Sensei steps in and blocks the action using an upward block (2). Then he moves to the side and grabs the opponent by the waist (3), throwing him onto the ground (4-5).

Muzila Sensei squares off against his opponent (1). The opponent initiates a sidekick attack. Muzila Sensei reacts by stepping in (2) and grabbing the aggressor by the leg and shoulder (3). Then he lifts him up (4) and smashes him on the ground (5), where he applies a punch to the face (6).

239

SEIJI NISHIMURA

WADO-RYU

Seiji Nishimura has a compiled a competition record that most people would envy. His impressive resume is the product of many years of hard and dedicated training. For more than a decade, he won virtually every major national and international tournament that he entered. He currently serves as a national coach for the Japan Karate-Do Federation and works as a professor at Fukuoka University, leading his students into a deeper understanding of the spiritual aspects of Budo. Nishimura himself is clearly a product of hard, relentless training. His cat-like movements are fast and smooth, and he also ahs the power of a thundering racehorse. His technique is impeccable and his combat timing is extremely precise.

Nishimura Sensei squares off against his opponent (1). When the opponent closes the distance using a mae-tsuki, Nishimura Sensei blocks the punch with his left hand (2) and counters with a right punch to the face (3). Then he brings his right leg behind the opponent's lead foot (4) and sweeps him (5). Once on the ground (6), Nishimura Sensei applies the final punch to the ribcage (7).

Nishimura faces his opponent (1). Nishimura Sensei closes the distance using a sweep feint as he simultaneously checks the opponent's left hand with his right hand (2). Then, without touching the floor with his right leg, he brings it to the front (3) and applies a jodan ura-mawashi-geri (4).

空手術

Nishimura Sensei squares off against his opponent (1). He closes the distance using an inside sweep feint and checks the opponent's left hand (2). He immediately lifts his leg and scores with a mawashi-geri to the face (3).

Seiji Nishimura faces his opponent (1). Nishimura Sensei closes the distance and grabs the opponent by the neck with his left hand (2). Then he throws him to the ground (3-4), where he applies the final punch (5).

245

Nishimura Sensei squares off against his opponent (1). When the opponent attacks with a mae-tsuki, Nishimura Sensei deflects the punch with his left hand and brings the right hand over the opponent's right shoulder (2). Then he steps in and brings his right elbow onto the opponent's chest (3) to apply a throw (4), which brings him to the ground (5), where Nishimura Sensei delivers a punch to the stomach (6).

Nishimura Sensei faces his opponent (1). The opponent attacks with a reverse punch to the midsection that Nishimura deflects with his left hand (2). He then counters with an ura-ken to the temple (3), followed by an inside sweep (4-5). This brings the opponent to the ground, where he finishes him off with a punch to the back (6).

EIHACHI OTA

SHORIN-RYU

In 1969, Sensei Ota moved to the United States. Despite being thousand of miles away from his roots, Ota kept training in the art he studied in his homeland. He sees karate-do not as sport but as a way of life, and he expects his students to also accept the art as part of Budo—not simply as a physical activity. In 1973, Sensei Ota opened his first dojo and hasn't stopped teaching since. An expert in the Okinawa weaponry art of kobudo, his life is based on the ethics of Budo, and he is a perfect example of a humble karate-do master. He is more interested in living a quiet life and sharing karate with his students than gaining fame and recognition in a modern world where the fundamental principles of ethics and honor are being forgotten.

Ota Sensei squares off against his opponent (1). The opponent attacks with a mae-tsuki that Ota counters with a left-hand parry and a right punch to the face (2), followed by mikazuki-geri to the face (3), a right elbow to the temple (4) and a throw (5). Once the opponent is on the floor, Ota Sensei (6) delivers a final punch to the face (7).

Ota Sensei faces the aggressor (1). When the opponent tries to grab Ota's lapels, he lifts both arms to break the attack (2) and drops into siko-dachi to apply shuto-uchi to the opponent's chest (3).

Ota Sensei faces his opponent (1). When the opponent attacks with mae-tsuki, Ota deflects the incoming punch with his right hand (2) and delivers a powerful gyaku-tsuki to the ribcage (3).

Ota Sensei squares off against his opponent (1). The opponent attacks with a reverse punch to the face, which is blocked by Ota's left hand (2). Then the aggressor tries a second punch that Ota Sensei blocks with his right hand (3). Immediately, Ota grabs the opponent's neck (4) and delivers an upward knee to the face (5).

Ota Sensei faces the aggressor (1). When the opponent tries to grab Ota's lapels, he lifts both arms to break the attack (2) and drops into a back stance to apply double tettsui-uchi to the opponent's ribcage (3).

Ota Sensei squares off against his opponent (1). The opponent attacks with a reverse punch that Ota blocks with an inside shuto-uke (2). Then he twists his right wrist and passes the opponent's attacking arm to the other side and simultaneously delivers an inverted finger jab to the eyes (3).

Ota Sensei faces the aggressor (1). When the opponent tries to grab Ota's lapels (2), he lifts both arms to break the attack (3) and drops into a horse stance to apply double tettsui-uchi to the opponent's ribcage (4), followed by a side punch to the chest (5) and a gyaku-tsuki to the face (6).

Ota Sensei squares off against his opponent (1). The opponent tries to grab Ota Sensei's left wrist; he reacts by reversing the grip and hitting the opponent's left elbow with his right forearm (2), which brings the opponent down (3).

The opponent faces Ota Sensei (1). He attacks with a mae-tsuki to the face that Ota Sensei deflects with his right hand (2) and counterattacks with a powerful reverse punch to the face (3).

Ota Sensei squares off against his opponent (1). The opponent attacks with a front kick that is deflected by Ota's right hand (2), and countered by a reverse punch (3), a front kick to the groin (4), an outside sweep to the lead leg (5) and a final punch to the face (6).

Ota Sensei faces the aggressor (1). The attacker grabs Ota's right wrist (2). Sensei reacts by reversing the grip (3), turning around and under the opponent's right arm (4), and throwing an elbow strike to the ribcage (5), followed by a punch to the side of the head (6-7).

Ota Sensei squares off against his opponent (1). The opponent attacks with a front kick that is blocked by Ota Sensei (2). The opponent continues the attack, but Ota Sensei intercepts it with both hands (3). Reversing the grips, Ota applies an armbar (4) and a final punch to the ribcage (5).

261

Ota Sensei faces his opponent (1). The opponent closes the distance (2) and attacks with a forward punch that is deflected by Ota's left hand (3), Then he counters with a ura-tsuki to the ribcage (4), followed by a stomping kick to the back of the opponent's right leg (5), and a final punch to the face (6).

Ota Sensei squares off against his opponent (1). The opponent tries to grab Ota Sensei, who moves back and creates distance (2) to counter with a strike to the face (3) and a straight vertical punch to the chin (4).

Ota Sensei faces the opponent (1). When the opponent tries to grab Ota with both hands, Sensei steps back and blocks both of the opponent's arms (2). He then grabs both sleeves and puts his left leg on the aggressor's left knee (3). He jumps and applies a downward elbow strike (4).

Ota Sensei squares off against his opponent (1). When the opponent tries to grab Ota's lapels, he steps back to create distance (2), grabs the opponent's head (3) and delivers an upward knee strike to the face (4).

RICHARD RABAGO

SHORIN-RYU

Richard Rabago has the experience, training credentials and Budo skill to have earned the right to be called "master" several times over. Trained by two of karate's most famous masters, Hidetaka Nishiyama and Tsuomu Ohshima, Rabago learned his most important lesson from them: Basics are everything. It wasn't until be met Tadashi Yamashita, though, that Rabago truly found his martial arts path in life. Applying the karate lessons of commitment, perseverance and mental training, Rabago insists that the most important lessons he can teach his students are not the physical ones, but the mental.

The attacker gets close to Rabago Sensei (1). As soon as the aggressor grabs Rabago's right wrist (2), Rabago Sensei moves his left leg back to create space, he moves his left hand over the opponent's left shoulder (3) and pushes downward to unbalance the opponent's position (4). Then he applies an upward knee strike (5), which brings the aggressor to the ground (6), where he finishes him off with a punch to the face (7).

The aggressor is ready to attack from behind (1). As soon as the aggressor closes the distance and touches Rabago Sensei shoulders, Rabago moves his arms forward to break the grip (2). Next, he moves his left leg forward, strikes the opponent's groin with a knife-hand strike (3) and follows with an elbow to the face (4).

The aggressor is ready to attack (1) and grabs Rabago Sensei from behind (2). Sensei moves his right leg to the side and lifts his right arm to break the grip (3). Then he grabs the opponent's right wrist and turns around (4) to apply a shuto-uchi to the back of the opponent's neck (5). Rabago Sensei finishes the opponent with an upward knee strike to the face (6).

Rabago Sensei faces his aggressor (1). When the opponent begins to push with both hands (2), Rabago Sensei attacks with both hands to the opponent's eyes (3). He follows with a double-knife hand strike to both sides of the opponent's neck (4) and a final palm strike to the chin with the right hand (5).

Rabago Sensei squares off against the opponent (1). The aggressor throws a punch that is blocked by Richard Rabago's left hand (2). Rabago Sensei then grabs the attacking arm and applies an elbow strike to the face (3). He moves his right hand around the opponent's neck (4) and brings him down (5-6) to the ground (7), where he gets ready (8) to apply the final punch to the face (9).

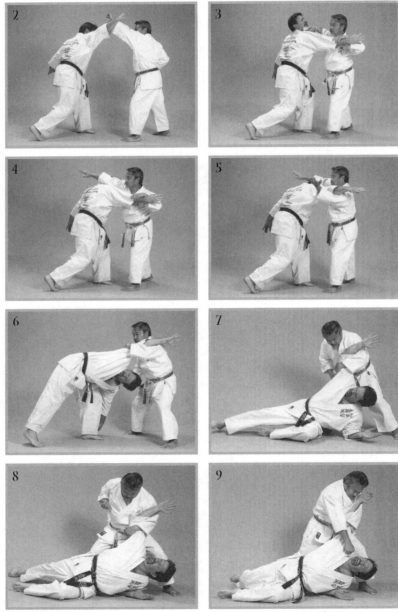

Rabago Sensei faces his aggressor (1). As soon as the aggressor grabs Rabago Sensei's lapels (2), Sensei reacts by controlling the grips with his left hand and delivering a finger jab to the opponent's eyes (3).

Rabago Sensei squares off against his opponent (1). When the opponent strikes with a left punch, Rabago Sensei blocks it with his left hand (2). Then he grabs the opponent's attacking arm with the right hand (3) and applies a punch to the ribcage (4). Immediately, Rabago Sensei turns around, hits the groin with a knife-hand strike (5) and finishes with an armbar (6).

The attacker gets close to Rabago Sensei and grabs him from behind (1-2). As soon as Rabago Sensei feels the grab, he moves his left leg back and applies a knife-hand strike to the opponent's groin (3), followed by a throw (4-5). Once the opponent is on the ground, Rabago Sensei (7) applies a final kick to the face (8).

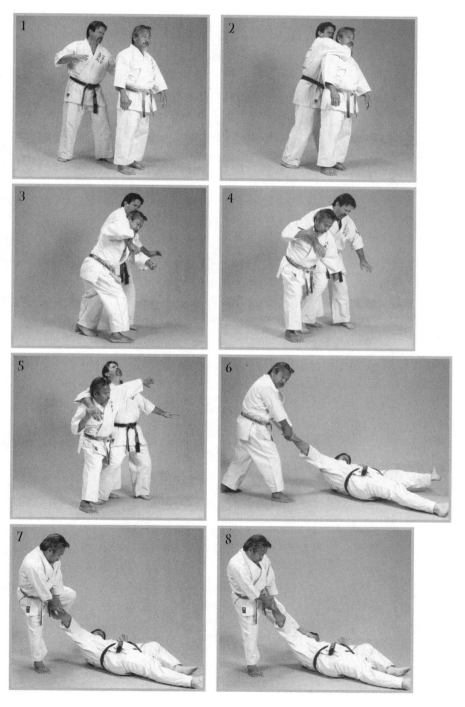

The opponent gets close and grabs Rabago's wrist from behind (1-2). Rabago Sensei steps to the side with his right leg as he simultaneously lifts his right arm (3). Then he turns around and brings his opponent to the front (4) to pass his left arm around the opponent's shoulder (5). Rabago Sensei moves his body to the left to apply a wristlock (6) and finishes with an upward knee strike to the chest (7).

Rabago Sensei faces his opponent (1). The opponent attacks with a punch that Rabago blocks with his left hand (2). Then he passes under the attacking arm (3), and without releasing the grip on the opponent's right wrist (4), applies an armbar (5) that brings the aggressor to the ground (6), where Rabago controls him (7).

277

The attacker gets close to Rabago Sensei (1) and grabs him from the side (2). Rabago hits the opponent's groin with his right hand (3), as he simultaneously pushes the face back with the left hand (4). This brings the opponent to the ground (5), where Rabago Sensei applies a shuto-uchi to the throat (6).

The aggressor grabs Richard Rabago's lapel (1). Rabago Sensei steps back to unbalance the opponent (2) and kicks him in the groin (3). Immediately, he turns to the right side and hooks the opponent's left arm (4) to apply a throw (6-7), which brings the aggressor to the ground (8), where Rabago Sensei delivers the final punch (9).

Rabago Sensei faces the opponent (1). The aggressor grabs both of Rabago's wrists (2). Rabago Sensei lifts both arms and kicks to the groin in one single action (3). Then he steps back to create distance (4) and applies an upward knee strike to the face (5).

The aggressor is trying to tackle Rabago Sensei (1). As soon as he grabs him (2), Rabago Sensei steps back with his left leg, hooks both arms (3) and applies a knee strike to the chest (4). Then he hits the opponent with an elbow strike to the back of the neck (5) and takes him down to the ground (6), where he can control him at will (7).

AVI ROKAH

SHOTOKAN

After training almost every day under Hidetaka Nishiyama for the past 20 years, Avi Rokah's technique and ability is absolutely second to none. His words have to be studied and not just read. Having the opportunity to train daily with a master of the magnitude and experience of Sensei Nishiyama is a once-in-a-lifetime opportunity, and Avi Rokah is well aware of this. Karate changed his life and gave him direction when he needed it the most. The art is in good and safe hands if it's to be passed onto future generations by people of Rokah's spirit, knowledge and technical level. He is, without a doubt, a special and elite karateka.

Sensei Rokah faces his opponent (1). When the attacker begins his assault, Avi Rokah slides his left foot and turns his back (2), creating distance to apply a back kick (3), which stops his opponent immediately (4).

Rokah Sensei squares off against his opponent (1). As the opponent attacks with a left punch, Rokah Sensei closes the distance and controls the opponent's left hand (2), so he can apply a final and decisive upward elbow strike to the chin (3).

285

Rokah faces his opponent (1). Sensei Rokah blocks a front kick attack with his left hand (2), steps back to create distance (3) and counters with a roundhouse kick to the mid-section (4-5).

Sensei Rokah faces his opponent (1). As soon as the attacker moves in (2), Rokah steps back and blocks with his left hand (3). Controlling the attacking arm (4), Rokah counters with a reverse punch (5).

Rokah Sensei faces his opponent (1). The opponent attacks with a front kick that Rokah deflects with his left hand (2). He then pushes the leg vigorously away to unbalance the aggressor (3). Then he counterattacks with a gyaku-tsuki to the opponent's back (4).

Rokah Sensei squares against his opponent (1). As the opponent initiates an attack by using a roundhouse kick, Rokah sidesteps to the right (2), creating distance to avoid the kick (3), and counterattacks with a reverse punch to the face (4).

ALEX STERNBERG

SHOTOKAN

Alex Sternberg, who began his martial arts training in 1963, started with a Korean style. He began teaching in 1966 and opened his own dojo in 1967. Selected as a member of the U.S. delegation to the World Championships since 1977, Sensei Sternberg has also published books and contributed articles and columns to international magazines around the world. A chief referee at many U.S. and international championships, Alex Sternberg currently teaches the art of karate-do in New York. With a determination to uphold the true spirit of karate, Sensei Sternberg has been one of the anchors of the modern shotokan movement and an example of the true meaning of Budo.

Both fighters have their left leg forward, squaring off (1). Sternberg Sensei sweeps from the outside with his right leg to the defender's left leg at a point just above the ankle (2). He moves his opponent's lead leg, unbalancing his stance (3), and immediately follows up with a jodan-tsuki (4).

Sensei Sternberg faces his opponent (1). He closes the distance and sweeps the inside of his opponent's left leg, momentarily throwing him off balance (2). Then he powers in with a jodan-gyaku-tsuki (3).

Sternberg Sensei faces his opponent (1). Sensei feints with a punch to close the distance and forces the defender to shift his weight to the right leg (2). Immediately, he places his right leg behind his opponent's legs and sweeps him, using his hip for a more powerful action (3).

Sternberg Sensei squares off with his opponent (1). As soon as his opponent begins to throw the roundhouse kick, Sensei Sternberg drops (2) and sweeps his opponent's supporting leg (3). Sternberg finishes with a kakato-geri on the chest (4-5).

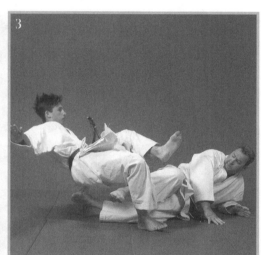

Sternberg Sensei faces his opponent (1). As his opponent throws a front kick, sensei steps to the left side and hooks the kicking leg using a sukui-uke (2). Then, he closes the distance, and using his hip and front leg, sweeps his opponent's supporting leg (3), finishing him off with a punch to the face (4).

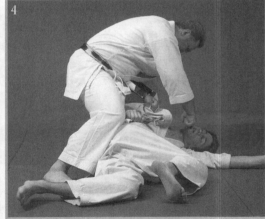

Sternberg Sensei faces his opponent (1). As soon as the opponent attacks, Sternberg Sensei blocks with his left hand (3) and punches with his right under the attacking arm (3). He follows with an elbow strike to the face (4).

297

Sternberg faces his opponent (1), who attacks with a mae-geri chudan that is blocked by Sternberg Sensei using a sukui-uke. He simultaneously sidesteps to the left (2-3) to finalize the counterattack with a reverse punch to the back of the neck (4).

Sternberg Sensei squares off against his opponent (1). The opponent attacks with a sidekick (2) that Sternberg evades and blocks with his right arm (3). He follows by hooking the attacking leg (4) and grabbing the aggressor's shoulder to pull him down (5) to the ground (6), where he finishes him off with a punch to the face (7).

299

KEIJI TOMIYAMA

SHITO-RYU

A direct student of founder Chojiro Tani, Tomiyama was chosen by Tani Sensei to spread the art in Europe according to the ethical and moral principles of the old Japanese traditions. Once known only for his ferocious fighting skills, Sensei Tomiyama has matured not only as a karate-ka but also as individual. With this maturity has come a philosophy that puts a proper perspective on when to fight and when not to fight. However, he still believes that there are times when a man must not retreat. Described as a teacher who gives as much as he demands, Tomiyama continues his dedicated task of spreading the message of his teacher.

Sensei Tomiyama faces his opponent (1). He starts punching with his right hand to close the distance (2), and follows with a left gyaku-tsuki (3), a left mawashi-geri jodan (4), a left ura-ken to the temple (5) and a right gyaku-tsuki to the mid-section (6).

Sensei Tomiyama squares off with Isaac Florentine (1). Florentine attacks with a gyaku-tsuki that is countered with a left-hand parry and a right-hand backfist to the temple (2). He follows with a front kick to the stomach (3) and a new gyaku-tsuki chudan (4). Using his right hand, Tomiyama Sensei throws his opponent to the ground (6), where he finishes with a punch to the mid-section (7).

Sensei Tomiyama faces his opponent (1). Tomiyama closes the distance with a sweep to the opponent's left leg (2), which disturbs his opponent's balance (3), and allows Tomiyama Sensei to turn 360 degrees (4), land a jodan ushiro-mawashi-geri (5), and follow with a gyaku-tsuki chudan (6).

Keiji Tomiyama faces his opponent (1). He stops his aggressor's attack with his left hand (2), grabs his neck with the left hand (3), and follows with a tetsui-uchi to the temple (4), a right elbow to the head (5), a downward ura-ken to the back of the neck (6), a front kick to the stomach (7), and a straight punch to the face (8).

Sensei Tomiyama waits for his opponent's attack (1). Tomiyama deflects the punch with a chudan-yoko-uke (2), hooks his left hand over his attacker's arms to apply an elbow wrench (3) and follows with an elbow strike to the face (4). He then applies a wristlock (5), followed by a palm strike to the groin (6-7).

Sensei Tomiyama faces his opponent (1). He blocks the attack with his left hand (2) and immediately counters with a nuki-te to the eyes (3), followed by a left finger jab to the throat (4). Tomiyama then drops and grabs his opponent's right leg (5), bringing him to the ground (6), where he finishes with a kakato-geri to the groin (7).

Tomiyama Sensei faces his opponent (1). As soon as the opponent attacks, Tomiyama Sensei steps back and controls the attacking arm (2). He follows with a tettsui-uchi to the face (3) and an elbow wrench with a stomp on the opponent's left foot (4 and detail).

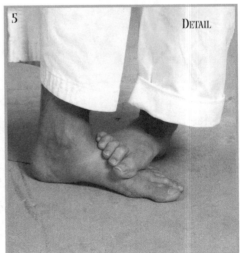

Tomiyama Sensei squares off against his opponent (1). The opponent attacks with a mae-tsuki that Sensei blocks with his left hand (2). Then he grabs the attacking arm (3) and applies a kin-geri to the stomach (4).

309

Keiji Tomiyama faces his opponent (1). The aggressor attacks with a reverse punch that is blocked by Tomiyama Sensei with his left hand (2). Then Sensei Tomiyama grabs the opponent's neck with his right hand (3) and delivers a knee strike to the opponent's chest (4).

Tomiyama Sensei squares off against his opponent (1). The opponent attacks with a reverse punch that is blocked by Tomiyama's left hand (2). Then he pushes the aggressor's attacking arm forward (3) to throw him off balance before (4) applying a final punch to the face (5).

311

Tomiyama Sensei faces his opponent (1). When the opponent steps in with a forward punch, Tomiyama Sensei creates distance and blocks the punch with his right hand (2) and simultaneously hits the opponent's elbow with his left arm (3). He follows with a final sidekick to the back of the knee (4-5).

Tomiyama Sensei faces his opponent (1). The aggressor throws a front kick that is blocked by Tomiyama Sensei (2). Sensei grabs the foot and twists it to the left (3), as shown in the detail photos (4-5). This brings the opponent to the ground (6), where Tomiyama Sensei applies a kick to the groin (7).

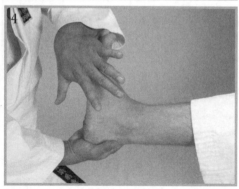

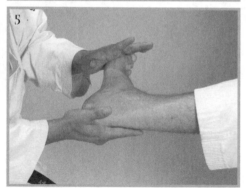

313

Keiji Tomiyama faces his opponent (1). When the opponent punches, Tomiyama Sensei sidesteps and blocks the punch with his right hand (2). Then he grabs the attacking arm, lifts it (3) and comes under it (4), so he can apply a backward elbow strike to the opponent's ribcage (5) and an elbow wrench (6).

Tomiyama Sensei squares off against his opponent (1). The opponent attacks with a forward punch that Tomiyama deflects using his right elbow (2). Then he uses his left hand to pass the attacking arm to the other side (3). This creates space to apply a stomping kick to the back of the leg (4), followed by a tettsui-uchi to the neck (5).

315

Keiji Tomiyama faces his opponent (1). Tomiyama Sensei initiates the attack by using his left hand to close the distance (2). He traps the opponent's blocking hand and applies a tettsui-uchi to the head (3). Then he grabs the opponent's neck, brings the head down (4) and applies a final elbow strike (5).

Tomiyama Sensei squares off against his opponent (1). The opponent attacks with a forward punch and Sensei evades the attack by sidestepping and using his left arm to block the strike (2). Then he brings his left leg inside the opponent's right leg (3), and using his left hand (4), pushes the opponent to the ground (5).

317

The opponent faces Tomiyama Sensei (1). Sensei deflects the incoming punch by using a mae-tsuki (2). Then he controls the attacking arm with his left hand (3) and applies a final punch to the opponent's face (4).

Tomiyama Sensei faces his opponent (1). The opponent attacks with a forward punch and Tomiyama Sensei uses a juji-uke to stop the strike (2). He then follows with a palm strike to the face (3), as he simultaneously controls the attacking arm (4).

Tomiyama Sensei squares off against his opponent (1). When the opponent attacks with a forward punch, Tomiyama Sensei uses an ude-uke to deflect the punch (2) and continues with a strike to the ribcage (3), followed by a right reverse punch to the face (4). Then he grabs the opponent's attacking arm and applies an armbar (5), which brings the aggressor to the ground for a final control (6).

Keiji Tomiyama faces his opponent (1). The opponent attacks with a forward punch to which Tomiyama Sensei reacts by blocking with an uchi-uke (2) and counterattacking with reverse punch to the chest (3). Then Sensei Tomiyama grabs the opponent's right wrist and applies a wristlock (5).

321

Tomiyama Sensei faces his opponent (1). He deflects the incoming attack by using an ude-uke (2). He follows that with a punch to the ribcage (3), a gyaku-tsuki to the head (4) and a final armbar to bring the opponent to the ground (5).

Tomiyama Sensei squares off against his opponent (1). When the opponent attacks with a forward punch (2), Tomiyama Sensei sidesteps, blocks with his left hand (3), grabs the wrist (3) and applies a wristlock to throw his opponent onto the ground (4).

TAMAS WEBER

SHITO-RYU

A decorated veteran of the French Foreign Legion, Tamas Weber has used karate-do to prevail in life-or-death combat situations and in the subtler occurrences of everyday life. Few people in the history of karate are more respected than Tamas Weber. Possessing a complete knowledge of karate lore and experience, Shihan Weber has put his life on the line on many occasions, in many wars, while serving with the French Foreign Legion. The bullet scars on his body punctuate his battlefield experience. It is in hard men like him that the true concept of life and death in the martial arts takes form.

Sensei Weber faces his opponent (1). The opponent attacks with a front kick that Weber Sensei blocks with his left hand (2). Then he uses both hands to block the incoming punch (3). He turns the blocking action into an armlock (4), followed by a front kick to the face (5), an outside sweep that brings the opponent down (6) and the final blow (7).

Sensei Weber squares off against his opponent (1). As soon as the opponent initiates his attack, Weber Sensei steps in and neutralizes the attack (2). He follows with a knee to the stomach (3) that brings the opponent to the ground (4), where Tamas Weber applies control with his right foot (5), and he finishes the opponent with a punch to the groin (6).

327

Tamas Weber faces his opponent (1). The opponent attacks with a forward punch that Weber Sensei blocks with his left hand (2). Then he uses an inside sweep to unbalance his opponent (3), followed by a palm strike to the face (4), a gyaku-tsuki to the stomach (5), and an outside sweep (6) to throw the opponent to the ground (7), where he finishes him with a punch to the ribcage (8).

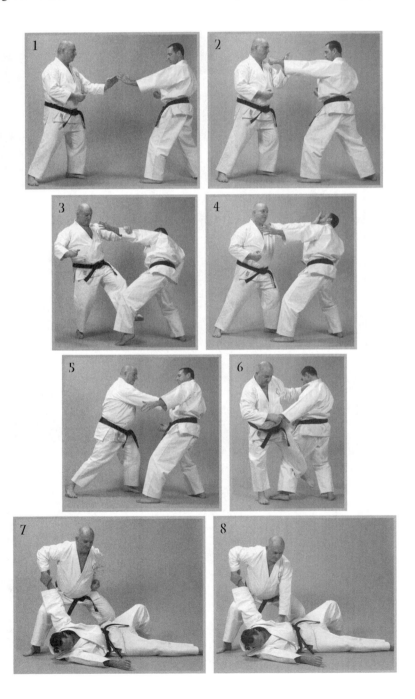

Weber Sensei squares off against his opponent (1). When the opponent initiates his attack with a left punch, Weber Sensei blocks it with a soto-uke (2), and he uses a gedan-barai to deflect the opponent's second attack (3). Immediately, he throws a reverse punch to the stomach as a counter (4), followed by an inside sweep to the opponent's left leg (5-6), which brings him to the ground (7) for the final punch (8).

329

KIYOSHI YAMAZAKI

RYOBU-KAI

Born in Chiba prefecture on 16 August 1940, Kiyoshi Yamazaki emigrated to the United States in 1968. Yamazaki Sensei has a reputation for outstanding technique and a deep knowledge of the Japanese traditions. His skill and proficiency has led to many jobs in the film industry as both an actor and technical adviser. As a prominent teacher, Yamazaki Sensei displays the qualities that are expected of a true master. He knows that a perfect balance can be achieved...a balance in which the art of karate-do becomes an international sport and—at the same time—maintains the true spirit and legacy of Budo.

空手術

Yamazaki Sensei squares off against his opponent (1). He steps in and punches his opponent in the face with a mae-tsuki (2), followed by a gyaku-tsuki to the stomach (3).

Yamazaki Sensei faces his opponent (1). Sensei steps in and scores with a mae-tsuki (2), followed by a reverse punch to the mid-section (3), an outside sweep (4) and a final punch to the ribcage (5).

333

Yamazaki Sensei squares off against his opponent (1). As soon as the opponent initiates the attack with a front kick, Yamazaki Sensei steps in and punches with a mae-tsuki jodan (2), followed by a haito-uchi to the temple (3).

Yamazaki Sensei lowers his position to draw the opponent's attack (1). As soon as the opponent initiates his kick, Yamazaki Sensei steps in and punches him in the face with a left mae-tsuki (2), followed by a gyaku-tsuki jodan (3).

Yamazaki Sensei squares off against his opponent (1). When the opponent steps straight in with a reverse punch, Yamazaki Sensei angles his body and uses a mae-tsuki to counter the action (2). Then he follows with a reverse punch to the face (3).

Yamazaki Sensei faces his opponent (1). The opponent attacks with a mae-tsuki jodan that is deflected by Sensei Yamazaki's left hand (2). Then he lifts his right knee (3) to counter with a roundhouse kick (4) to the opponent's body (5).

Yamazaki Sensei squares off against his opponent (1). As soon as the opponent initiates his kick (2), Yamazaki Sensei steps in and anticipates the attack with his mawashi-geri chudan (3). Then he brings his right foot down (4), turns around and applies a final ushiro-ura-mawashi-geri to the face (5).

Yamazaki Sensei squares off against his opponent (1). The opponent attacks with a front kick. Yamazaki Sensei simultaneously reacts to the attack by sidestepping and punching with a gyaku-tsuki jodan (2).

Yamazaki Sensei faces his opponent (1). The opponent attacks with a mae-tsuki that is deflected by Sensei's left hand (2). Then he blocks the incoming gyaku-tsuki with the same hand (3), and pushes the attacking arm away to unbalance the opponent (4), so he can counterattack with a reverse punch to the ribcage (5).

Yamazaki Sensei squares off against his opponent (1). He blocks the opponent's mawashi-geri jodan (2) and follows with a front kick to the stomach (3). Before the opponent lands, Yamazaki Sensei sweeps the attacking leg (4), bringing him to the ground (5), where he can easily (6) apply the final punch (7).

Yamazaki Sensei faces his opponent (1). The opponent charges with a front kick that Yamazaki Sensei blocks with his left hand (2). The opponent then throws a roundhouse kick with the left leg that is blocked by Sensei's right hand (3). Then Yamazaki Sensei brings his right knee up (4) to apply a counterattack using an ura-mawashi-geri jodan (5).

Yamazaki Sensei squares off against his opponent (1). The opponent initiates his attack with a roundhouse kick to the face that is blocked by Yamazaki (2). Yamazaki Sensei brings his body down and spins as the opponent turns (2) to throw an ura-mawashi-geri (3). From the bottom, Yamazaki Sensei sweeps the opponent's supporting leg (6), bringing him down to the ground (6), where he scores with a kick to the stomach (7).

343

Yamazaki Sensei faces his opponent (1). Sensei initiates the attack using a mae-tsuki, but the opponent blocks the technique with his left hand (2) and counterattacks with a reverse punch (3) and a roundhouse kick to the face that is blocked by Yamazaki Sensei (4). Then, Sensei Yamazaki brings his left knee up to hit the opponent's inside calf (5). He brings the left foot down (6) to establish position to apply an inside sweep (7). He then takes the opponent to the ground (8) for a final kick to the groin (9).

Yamazaki Sensei squares off against his opponent (1). As a distraction, Sensei steps in and feints with an outside sweep to the opponent's left leg (2) and then follows with a mawashi-geri jodan (3).

Karate's Finest Masters Teach

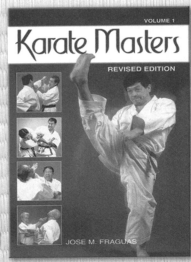

KARATE MASTERS Vol.1 (Revised Edition)
By Jose M. Fraguas

Through conversations with many historical figures such as Osamu Ozawa, Teruo Hayashi, Kenzo Mabuni, Masatoshi Nakayama, and numerous current world-class masters such as Hirokazu Kanazawa, Fumio Demura, Takayuki Mikami, Teruyuki Okazaki, Morio Higaonna, Hidetaka Nishiyama, James Yabe, Tak Kubota, Bill Dometrich, Dan Ivan, and Stan Schmidt, the many threads of karate learning, lore, and legend are woven together to present an integrated and complete view of the empty-handed art of fighting, philosophy, and self-defense. Containing information that has not appeared anywhere else, the interviews contain intriguing thoughts, fascinating personal details, hidden history, and revealing philosophies.
#110 - $19.95 – 7 x 10 – 350 pages
ISBN: 978-1-933901-22-0

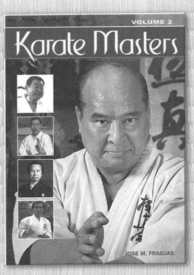

KARATE MASTERS Vol. 2
By Jose M. Fraguas

The second volume of the series offers a new repertoire of historical figures, such as Mas Oyama, Kyoshi Yamazaki. Masahiko Tanaka, Eihachi Ota, Yukiyoshi Marutani, Randall Hassell, Keinosuke Enoeda, Richard Kim, Shinpo Matayoshi, Tsutomu Ohshima, Yoshiaki Ajari, Goshi Yamaguchi, and other world-recognized professional martial artists. In this volume, new interviews with the world's top karate masters have been gathered to present an integrated and complete view of the empty-handed art of fighting, philosophy, and self-defense.
 # 111 - $29.95 – 7 x 10 – 350 pages
ISBN: 978-1-933901-20-9

TO ORDER VISIT: www.empirebooks.net

Budo Greatest Lessons

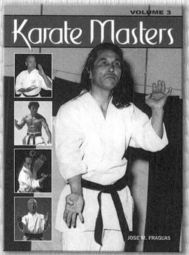

KARATE MASTERS Vol.3
By Jose M. Fraguas

Including twenty-three exclusive interviews with legendary masters, such as Gogen "The Cat" Yamaguchi, Teruo Chinen, Edmond Otis, Akio Minakami, Jiro Ohtsuka, Shojiro Koyama, Ryusho Sakagami, Katsutaka Tanaka, Anthony Mirakian, Tetsuhiko Asai, Mikio Yahara, and other karate giants, this volume contains intriguing thoughts, fascinating personal details, hidden histories, and inspiring philosophies, as each master reveals his true love for the art and a deep understanding of every facet associated with the practice and spirit of the Japanese art of Karate-do as a way of life. This invaluable reference book is a "must have" addition to your personal library.

112 - $29.95 – 7 x 10 – 350 pages
ISBN: 978-1-933901-04-6

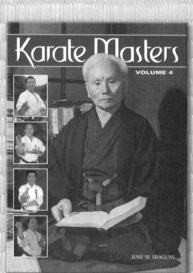

KARATE MASTERS Vol.4
By Jose M. Fraguas

After the acclaimed success of the first three volumes of Karate Masters, the author proudly presents "Karate Masters 4", with a new repertoire of historical figures, such as Yutaka Yaguchi, Hiroyasu Fujishima, Takeshi Uchiage, Kenneth Funakoshi, Kunio Murayama, Shoji Nishimura, Hiroshi Okazaki, Gene Tibon, Les Safar, Koss Yokota, Richard Amos, Taku Nakasaka, and other world-recognized Karate masters like George E. Mattson, Joe Carbonara, Tony Annesi, etc…. In this fourth volume, new interviews with the world's top Karate masters have been gathered to present an integrated and complete view of the empty-handed art of fighting, philosophy, and self-defense. Containing information that has not appeared anywhere else, the interviews contain intriguing thoughts, fascinating personal details, hidden history, and revealing philosophies as each master reveals his true love for the art and a deep understanding of every facet associated with the practice and spirit of the Japanese art of Karate-do as a way of life. It's a detailed reference work, and a "must have" addition to your personal library.

#133– $29.95 – 7 x 10 – 370 pages
ISBN: 978-1-933901-49-7

伝統空手